THE **POWER**
OF **TEACHING**
VULNERABLY

HOW RISK-TAKING TRANSFORMS STUDENT ENGAGEMENT

FOREWORD BY KATHERINE BOMER

DAVID ROCKOWER

HEINEMANN
PORTSMOUTH, NH

Heinemann

145 Maplewood Avenue, Suite 300

Portsmouth, NH 03801

www.heinemann.com

Offices and agents throughout the world

Library of Congress Cataloging-in-Publication Data

Names: Rockower, David, author.

Title: The power of teaching vulnerably : how risk-taking transforms student engagement / David Rockower.

Description: Portsmouth, NH : Heinemann 2021. | Includes bibliographical references.

Identifiers: LCCN 2021025747 | ISBN 9780325135236

Subjects: LCSH: Composition (Language arts)—Study and teaching. | English language—Composition and exercises—Study and teaching. | Teacher–student relationships.

Classification: LCC LB1575.8 .R63 2021 | DDC 428.0071—dc23

LC record available at https://lccn.loc.gov/2021025747

Editor: Heather Anderson

Production: Vicki Kasabian

Text and cover designs: Monica Ann Cohen

Typesetting: Gina Poirier Design

Manufacturing: Val Cooper

Printed in the United States of America on acid-free paper

1 2 3 4 5 VP 25 24 23 22 21

September 2021 Printing

TO MICHELLE, NATHAN, AND MADDIE . . . MY INSPIRATIONS

TO THE DELTA PROGRAM . . . YOU SAVED ME AS A STUDENT
AND AGAIN AS A TEACHER.

CONTENTS

ACKNOWLEDGMENTS

During my first year as a teacher, I met a colleague who was months away from retirement. She loved teaching elementary school, but after almost forty years in the classroom, it was time to move on. She reminded me that teaching children is a gift and that she couldn't imagine another job where she could come to work every day and be surrounded by people who begged her to read them stories, who asked unfiltered questions, whose curiosities would drive conversations, who would occasionally leave notes on her desk that brought her to tears. She acknowledged that I would, no doubt, be on a roller coaster of a career. But oh, she said, what fun! She was right.

I would like to thank all of my mentors along the way, those who reminded me to always find the good in every student and taught me that we have a choice between focusing on what frustrates us about our students or recognizing their strengths and building them up. To the authors whose books have influenced my teaching, Katherine Bomer, Nancie Atwell, Donalyn Miller, Alfie Kohn, and Tom Newkirk: thank you for continuing to guide my practice. Though I've never met Brené Brown, her vulnerability work inspired me to investigate how leaning into discomfort impacts teaching and learning.

The Heinemann Fellows in cohort three pushed and supported me in all the right ways. Special thanks to Julie Jee and Irene Castillon—you were the most kind and encouraging research partners. Ellin Oliver Keene read my rambling blogs during my action research project; thank you for helping to refine my focus. Sonja Cherry-Paul's feedback regarding dialogic vulnerability helped reframe my thinking and challenged me to engage in identity work. Thank you. Vicki Boyd, Mim Easton, Roderick Spelman, and Stephen Perepeluk: thank you for showing interest in my work and for your kindness throughout the process. Thanks to Katie Wood Ray for the long phone conversations and reflective email responses during my fellowship. Your probing questions and wise observations were just what I needed.

To my editor, Heather Anderson, thank you for your patience and the magical way you nudged me to restructure the book. When it felt like too much, you made it all seem doable. As a first-time author who, at times, felt out of his element, I relied on your guidance and positivity.

Thanks to editorial coordinator Krysten Lebel, production editor Vicki Kasabian, Monica Ann Cohen in design, and Kim Cahill in marketing. Please know how much I value your creativity and care.

Thanks to all of the teachers who agreed to share their stories here. Dana Ciciliot, Paul McCormick, Jen Rand, Leah Mueller, Kate Walker, Virginia Squier, Michael Goldfine, and Dot Burnett: thank you for your vulnerability and authenticity. Special thanks to Paul, who is the embodiment of a vulnerable teacher; your practice inspires me daily. Thank you, Jon Downs, for encouraging healthy risk-taking, and for allowing us to lead together.

A long conversation with Anne Whitney helped me hone my research question. At a time when I was questioning my intent and struggling to focus, your wisdom allowed me to dive back in with renewed energy. Thank you, Anne.

To all of my students: you are everything, the reason we do what we do. Thanks to the students of Delta Middle who contributed their time and energy to this book. Without their written responses and interviews, this book would not exist. Thanks to the parents who shared their perspectives; no one knows our students better than you do; including your voice is critical.

Mom and Dad, thanks for your encouragement and love. From a very early age, my mother demonstrated that school didn't have to be the way it's always been. Her progressive outlook on learning and school pushed me to reimagine the way we teach.

Finally, I thank my wife, Michelle, for her support and encouragement. You always listen with deep interest to my stories, questions, and frustrations. And Nathan and Maddie—your love keeps me moving forward.

FOREWORD

THE OFFER OF VULNERABILITY AND TRUST IS PRECIOUS,
SOMETHING WE AS TEACHERS TREASURE—IT HELPS MAKE
POSSIBLE A RELATIONSHIP WHERE BOTH GIVER AND
RECEIVER BENEFIT. IT'S A BIG PART OF THE REASON WE
ALL WANTED TO BECOME TEACHERS IN THE FIRST PLACE.

—THOMAS NEWKIRK, *EMBARRASSMENT AND
THE EMOTIONAL UNDERLIFE OF LEARNING*

With *The Power of Vulnerability*, David Rockower could well become our very own and much-adored Brené Brown for teachers. In his clear, honest, and beautiful prose, he tells the story of his personal journey toward becoming a more responsive and empathetic teacher—more willing to admit mistakes and doubts, to apologize (without defense) to his students, and to take risks in his classroom, like sharing early drafts of his own writing about emotional experiences or doing personal identity work before inviting students to have difficult conversations about race, equity, and white privilege. David argues convincingly that vulnerable teaching is not only liberating for the teacher, but actually results in more eager, engaged learning in students. He provides a remarkably rich road map, reinforced by testimonials from students, colleagues, and guardians about the power of vulnerability, and he guides us step-by-step through actions we can take to become more vulnerable, more human, and therefore, more effective teachers with our own students.

Frankly, I admire the risk David takes to write a book about vulnerability, a concept that is, like the varied tastes and textures of fine wine, hard to describe, to pinpoint, but something that you know when you taste and feel it. Every teacher remembers a time—perhaps during an impromptu discussion following a traumatic event, or when everyone burst into laughter over a pigeon seeming to admire its reflection in the window, or when a particularly moving passage in a read-aloud book caused many in the class to cry openly, or when a student beamed after hearing a specific, heartfelt compliment about their writing—when they feel that tingling in the skin and change of air in the room that says something real and true was just born. We can't plan for those moments because they can only happen inside trusting relationships, in the midst of living together in the classroom. They happen when we open our hearts, and when we are honest about what we think and feel. They happen when we look closely and listen deeply to our students. They are often the moments (sometimes the only moments) that students remember about our time together, even years later.

For those who might think the scenarios I just described are not the purpose of education, that school exists to teach children those practical, hard skills that will get them into college and lead to lucrative careers, think again. The days of silent students perched in rows, performing in obedience to the lesson and the textbook are over. Even before the COVID-19 pandemic, educators knew that the technologies, workspaces, and challenges of the twenty-first century require different ways of teaching and learning that incorporate so-called soft skills such as compassion, conversation, collaboration, and critical perspective-taking. During the lockdown, everyone—teachers, kids, and their families at home—had to learn new ways of doing school in virtual spaces. There were plenty of bumps on that road, on everyone's part, but the adults and kids who got through it best were those who could admit how hard it all was and ask for help. As we came back to be in community with one another inside school buildings, we knew we needed to build rituals of caring and constant checking in on one another so that we might heal after such physical, emotional, and social disruption. But the truth is, we always need those qualities if we want to create safe, vibrant learning spaces. Thankfully, David's book bears out the benefits of a more vulnerable teaching stance, and it overflows with possibilities for structures and activities that fashion and foster a joyful community. The classrooms and school that David describes are places where students feel seen, heard, and especially, necessary. Students learn how to talk to each other and read each other's work to cheerlead and offer constructive suggestions. They learn how to navigate brave conversations about crucial topics. Students take on leadership roles that have genuine impacts in the school community and beyond.

We need to understand, of course, that vulnerability is not a curriculum kit we can purchase—it's not a canned unit we can pull out every October. As David points out, the readiness for extreme vulnerability will vary according to the students in each classroom. Instead, we must authentically nurture an atmosphere of trust and compassion, bit by bit. It might begin, as it did for David, in our own storytelling or with a frank piece of writing. Just as we model how to structure an essay, how to experiment with line breaks in a poem, or how to cite sources in a paper, we can demonstrate how to write honestly, with specificity and voice. From there, we can practice any of the myriad ways David offers for exploring and exhibiting vulnerability in teaching and learning: writing conferences, critical conversations, identity presentations, whole-school community meetings, and quarterly schoolwide talent showcases. It is especially helpful to learn that timing matters when deciding to showcase vulnerability. Boundaries are necessary so that people will not experience emotional harm, and David teaches us how to build relationships that can sustain some difficult truths.

What shines brightly throughout David's book is how much he loves teaching, and how much he loves his students, and I believe that if we all felt and behaved this way, we would make a better world. But for anyone who might worry that love is beside the point, or that a vulnerability discourse feels frivolous in the face of standards, tests, and evaluations, I suggest heading straight to the Appendix to relish the samples of David's students' work that should satisfy any anxiety about fulfilling achievement goals. As a fellow teacher of writing, I know we can only realize this confident, richly textured, and engaging quality of writing when students feel safe, seen, and cherished in their classroom. Indeed, this feeling of trust and caring is precious, for us as well as for our students, and isn't this what called us to teaching?

—Katherine Bomer

INTRODUCTION

TEACHING AND LEARNING AS A VULNERABLE ACT

ONE LOOKS BACK WITH APPRECIATION TO THE BRILLIANT
TEACHERS, BUT WITH GRATITUDE TO THOSE WHO
TOUCHED OUR HUMAN FEELINGS. THE CURRICULUM
IS SO MUCH NECESSARY RAW MATERIAL, BUT
WARMTH IS THE VITAL ELEMENT FOR THE GROWING
PLANT AND FOR THE SOUL OF THE CHILD.

—CARL JUNG

With a dry throat, shaky hands, and hammering heart, I stood in front of my fifth-grade classmates, anxious to get out of the spotlight. I'd rehearsed my speech at home, but no amount of practice could prepare me for the twenty-five eleven-year-olds whose judging eyes bore through my chest. The teacher thought she was being helpful when she said, "David, try to relax. We are all friends here." This made things worse, as it brought even more attention to the fact that I was nervous. I stumbled (and mumbled) through the presentation, then hurried back to my seat. I'm sure there were some sympathetic smiles that I misinterpreted as smirks. But several classmates openly mocked my fear, which turned my embarrassment into anger. I do remember our teacher praising many of the presenters who followed for their composure, their loud, confident voices. Each compliment stung, reminding me how I was not good enough. Needless to say, that classroom was not an emotionally safe space for me. The classroom culture was competitive, and the teacher attempted to use fear as a motivational tool. Thankfully, the next school year was much different.

At the end of our sixth-grade year, each student was to deliver a long presentation on a topic of our choosing. Baseball was my life at the time, and the

Philadelphia Phillies were my favorite team. I decided to research the history of baseball and bring in my personal passion for the Phillies. I can still remember the giant note cards and how I'd repeatedly sharpened my Ticonderoga pencil to make sure each word was legible; the Phillies poster with Steve Carlton and Mike Schmidt, one holding a flaming baseball, the other a flaming bat; the royal blue V-neck sweater I wore; the smile on my teacher's face as she cheered me on throughout the presentation. I actually enjoyed the process, and I was beyond proud of myself when it was over.

How could two presentations, one year apart, result in completely different emotional responses and experiences? This was not a simple lesson in learning from a fifth-grade flop and "trying harder" the following year—I prepared equally for both assignments. Each required me to take a risk, to complete a task that made me uncomfortable. But one occurred in a competitive, divisive environment, and the other took place in an emotionally safe space.

I never thought I would become a teacher. I generally disliked school and did what I had to do to get by. But there were teachers along the way who inspired me and made me feel important. Everything that was bad about school—the mindless work, the bullying, the focus on compliance—all but disappeared when I was under the care of my favorite teachers. Though those classes could be boisterous, the learning environment was authentic. It was messy, frustrating at times but engaging. It often seemed more like home, where I felt empowered to speak my mind, push back, and share my frustrations. In those classrooms, I was able to be myself, or at least, mix it up with other people my age, people like me who were trying to figure out what they really believed in, what drove them to actually *want* to solve a math problem or pick up a book on their own.

My favorite teachers all had one thing in common: They were risk-takers. They would stop a lesson to talk about what was on our mind; they grappled with ideas alongside us; they played four square and laughed with us during recess; they looked us in the eye and apologized when they messed up; they showed us who they were outside of the classroom; they were flexible with the curriculum; they got to know us and found something beautiful in every student. When I decided to become a teacher, I wanted to harness everything those teachers taught me about being human. I wanted my classroom to be a second home, and I wanted the work to matter. Unfortunately, it didn't happen as quickly as I would have liked.

The first time I taught poetry, I was nervous. I had little experience with the genre and didn't have anything worth sharing with my students. Honestly, I wanted to get through the unit because it felt uncomfortable. So I set up stations. At each station I had directions and examples. Station 1 was concrete poetry; station 2, acrostic poetry; station 3, limerick; and so on. This was brilliant! Students could teach themselves; all I needed to do was move around the room, encouraging, asking questions, and helping them generate ideas. This required some preplanning but once things got going, there would be little to no risk on my part. The unit turned out just fine. The kids wrote sterile, risk-free, predictable poems. There was no voice, no heart, but I was pleased, because, hey, they wrote poems. I could check that box off my curricular to-do list. Thankfully, that new-teacher acceptance of surface-level learning didn't last.

Each school year, I nudged myself toward more authenticity in the classroom. As I grew as a teacher, it became too painful to simply go through the motions, checking off boxes. If I didn't feel energy from the students, if I saw tired, compliant eyes, I became restless. And at some point, I realized that the required change was not the tweaking of lesson plans, but rather the revealing of myself as a human being who did all the things I was asking them to do in school. I needed to show them that I wrote and read and struggled to find engagement in school. I needed to reveal what went through my head when staring at a blank sheet of paper. How did I organize my thoughts before writing? How many times did I tear up a draft and begin again? How often did I abandon a book—sometimes because I didn't like it, and sometimes because I didn't understand it? It was time to stop acting like a teacher who knew all the answers, and time to start revealing the fallible adult in the room who grappled with self-doubt, who wrote bad poetry, who sometimes still struggled to focus.

A few years later, with the poetry unit looming, I knew I needed to do more than create stations. I made a commitment to write my own poetry. I cringed as I wrote, revised, and edited. I kept every draft. It wasn't great, but it was real. I wrote about some of my failures and successes in school, specific moments on the playground that I'd never forget. I wrote one poem about the time I ran away from home when I was seven years old—when I filled my backpack with granola bars, grabbed my pillow, and made it to the end of the block before stopping to consider where I might go. I wrote about sitting down on the curb while pondering my options. And I wrote about running home to hug my parents.

When I read those poems aloud to my students, I remember being surprised at how exposed I felt. I was sharing part of my life, but I was also revealing my attempt at this particular art form. I felt uneasy because these were not particularly good poems, and I didn't want to model something, well . . . *bad*. But the response from my students was unexpected. They asked questions and wanted to share their own stories: "Why did you run away?" "What did your parents do when you got back?" "Hey, I did the same thing, but I made it all the way to the park!" I showed them my drafts and how I struggled with trying to say what I wanted without sounding forced or cliché. I explained that we'd be writing free-verse poetry and that they didn't need to worry about rhyming. They should focus on revealing memorable moments. "Take us into some of the big and little events from your life," I told them. Show us the color and condition of your sneakers from third grade, invite us to hear the sound of your best friend's laugh.

And that's when the students began writing their own poems—for themselves, about themselves. They were (as Jacqueline Woodson defines poetry) finding "joy and urgency in tiny spaces" (Ray 2006, 205). For the first time, they were writing from the heart. They wrote about how the stitches of a well-worn baseball made them feel alive, how the smell of coffee in the morning reminded them of their father, how shelter from an August thunderstorm brought them the same comfort as a hug from their grandmother. For the first time, the writing was real, and I was done with stations.

Reflecting on this experience, it's clear to me that my willingness to be vulnerable, to take a risk, to not only show them my own struggles with the craft of writing but also let them see that I was afraid to share, opened the door for my students to engage in real learning.

We routinely ask our students to take emotional risks in school. Their mere presence in a room with twenty-some classmates guarantees moments of discomfort and uncertainty. And we know that when these moments occur in an environment that is grounded in acceptance, care, and support, we increase the chances for positive student growth and meaningful learning. Student risk-taking in school is inevitable and important. How, then, can we ask our students to take risks when we, as teachers, do not? If students learn best from modeled behavior, shouldn't teachers be required to lean into uncertainty alongside students?

I played it emotionally safe for my first few years of teaching. It was scary enough to be responsible for the well-being and education of a classroom full of students—the idea of revealing my own fears, doubts, successes, and failures was not even on my radar. But it should have been. I was asking them to write personal essays, argue, persuade, and share their art with others. All of these tasks require emotional risk. In time, I learned that to help my students discover what matters most to them, and to use those passions as catalysts to impactful learning, I needed to step up, lean out over the edge, and take the leap into teacher vulnerability.

THREE DIMENSIONS **OF** TEACHER VULNERABILITY

THE DIFFICULT THING IS THAT VULNERABILITY IS
THE FIRST THING I LOOK FOR IN YOU AND THE LAST
THING I'M WILLING TO SHOW YOU. IN YOU, IT'S
COURAGE AND DARING. IN ME, IT'S WEAKNESS.

—BRENÉ BROWN, "THE POWER OF VULNERABILITY"

In 2010, researcher, speaker, and author Brené Brown gave what would become one of the most-watched TED Talks of all time. She spoke about the power of vulnerability and why we should choose courage over comfort. Her words resonated with me and changed the way I think about leaning into discomfort. She defines vulnerability as "uncertainty, risk, and emotional exposure" (Brown 2010). I started to think about school and how often we ask students to walk into uncertainty, risk, and emotional exposure (every day!). But what about teachers? What about me?

I think many of us protect ourselves from emotional exposure. Often, our need to appear confident and competent and in control prevents us from taking risks. But how can we ask our students to be vulnerable if we aren't modeling it ourselves? Certainly, there are limits; we can't overshare, and we need to be sensitive to the personal experiences of our students. But I think we can invite opportunities to take risks.

As I thought about Brown's definition of vulnerability, I began to wonder what actions I'd taken (or avoided taking) as a teacher that required uncertainty, risk, and emotional exposure. I reflected on the stories I told my students, and how they loved to hear about my childhood adventures. Though I typically stuck to safe stories, I would occasionally dip my toe into something that made me a bit uneasy: the loss of a close grandparent, how I was embarrassed by my principal in first grade, and what it was like to be one of the only Jewish boys in my school. Over time, I began to talk more about my hobbies outside of school. Students enjoyed hearing about my bread-baking adventures, and of course, tasting some of my homemade sourdough loaves. They thought it was cool when I showed them my first 5K race results—even though (or maybe especially because) several of them finished well ahead of me. Sharing these stories required personal vulnerability.

I also looked back at the times I regretted saying something to a student or a whole class. I'd go home feeling guilty for taking out my frustrations on everyone instead of looking inward. When I had a class that was consistently off-task, I made it about the students, tried to explain how they were being disrespectful. Had I been honest with myself, I would have recognized the fact that I may have been boring them, and some of them might have been dealing with personal struggles. Instead, I pulled one of the boisterous students aside and scolded them for their behavior. In the car on the way home, I'd shake my head, wishing I'd handled it differently. That self-reflection was important, and it eventually led to a change in how I viewed "misbehavior." I'm now better able to see those behaviors as warning signs, telling me that I need to adjust my lesson, tone, or word choice. It also forced me to think about apologizing. We are always encouraging our students to apologize for their mistakes, but how often are teachers willing to do this? I couldn't think of many times when I'd offered a genuine apology to a student—doing so requires relational vulnerability.

Finally, I considered how often I'd shied away from crucial conversations in the classroom. There were plenty of times when students asked questions about topics that made me feel uncomfortable. I was ill prepared to lead these discussions—either because I was afraid that their guardians wouldn't want them talking about certain topics in school or because I wasn't well enough informed to lead such a conversation. I'm sure I said something like, "That's important, but you should talk to your parents about it." At the time, I thought I was doing the right thing, but in reality, I was only trying to protect my ego. I convinced myself that the issues were "too political" or "not appropriate" for the age group. But what might we have all learned from one another after dialoguing about the topic? I would never know, because I was too scared of retribution. That was foolish. I've since come to real-ize that some of the best conversa-tions in my classroom occur when I've invited students to talk about class, race, LGBTQIA+, and equity issues. This has required me to look inward, examine my own biases, read, research, and find colleagues or community members to help me prepare for and lead these conversations. Engaging in critical conversations requires dialogic vulnerability.

After reflecting on my twenty-three years as a classroom teacher and spending the last two conducting an action research project in my classroom around this idea, I believe that teacher vulnerability helps to establish strong student–teacher relationships, breaks down hierarchies, builds trust, increases student engagement, and provides the foundation for a healthy school culture.

Teacher Identity and Relationships

When I started teaching, there was a confident, risk-taking teacher down the hall from me. I watched her in awe, wondering how she so naturally swept up her class in stories about trips to the doughnut shop or learning to ride a tractor. She found a way to connect everything she taught to stories. And it wasn't just about her; she'd talk about geology and make a connection to one of her student's hobbies. It was magical to watch and also a bit intimidating. How could I possibly teach at that level? What I didn't realize at the time was that all of her risks, her silliness, her wild stories, occurred because of her willingness to be vulnerable.

Yet, I was not ready to make so many mistakes, to be so transparent and casual in front of the class. I needed more time, I thought. More time to figure out who I was as a teacher, more time to nail down the curriculum. This was backward thinking. I tried to loosen up, tell a story, and be like this veteran superstar. At first, it felt uncomfortable, and I drove home embarrassed. But the more flexible and real I was with my teaching, the more I enjoyed school, and so, it seemed, did my students. Looking back, I now understand that although I saw that dynamic teacher's vulnerability as courage and strength, I saw my own vulnerability as a weakness.

I eventually learned from this teacher, and all my role models, that relationships are everything. As a student, I learned the most important lessons from teachers who (I knew) cared about me. As a teacher, I've learned the most from colleagues who consistently demonstrate to their students how much they care about all aspects of their lives. We cannot develop these kinds of deep connections with students unless we are willing to show them who we are. Telling our stories, being open and honest, listening deeply, and engaging in real conversations are necessary ingredients for an authentic classroom.

When we lean into uncertainty, risk, and emotional exposure in school, it can occur in a variety of forms. We might share the fact that we're struggling to stay focused because something's weighing on our mind, engage in a one-on-one conversation with a student to explain why their words were hurtful, or introduce a topic for discussion that may create discomfort. Each of these requires us to take a risk but falls into a different category. I've identified three common types or dimensions of teacher vulnerability: personal, relational, and dialogic.

Personal Vulnerability

I describe personal stories, whether oral or written, as those that *share a failure, joy, or a memorable moment.* They might also include sharing artistic work or hobbies.

After a few years in the classroom, I began to feel comfortable talking about my history with students. I enjoyed sharing stories about childhood, failed hobbies, embarrassing moments. Each year, when teaching a memoir unit, I tell the story about how I fell from a rope swing when I was twelve. I tell it quickly the first time, leaving out all the little moments and tidbits that made the memory so scary. Next, I ask what questions students have, and there are many. Finally, I retell the story in great detail. They hang on every word, laughing at first, and then covering their faces when they know that the rope was about to snap.

There is no better community-building activity than personal storytelling. When teachers open up and share the specifics of a life event, students are engaged, and often, their hands shoot up and they want to tell similar stories. Want to hear about every student's bruised knee, broken bone, and bloody elbow? Tell a story about the time you broke your arm, and you are guaranteed to have middle schoolers waving their arms, desperately needing to share their own tales.

My story about falling from the rope swing did not require much personal vulnerability. I don't have an emotional reaction when retelling it now, but it resonates with students and works well as a model for memoir writing. However,

LOOKING BACK, I NOW UNDERSTAND THAT ALTHOUGH I SAW THAT DYNAMIC TEACHER'S VULNERABILITY AS COURAGE AND STRENGTH, I SAW MY OWN VULNERABILITY AS A WEAKNESS.

there have been other teaching moments when I've felt moved to share something that sparks an emotional reaction, or at least surprised me while writing about it.

A quote from Robert Frost hangs in my classroom: "No tears in the writer, no tears in the reader. No surprise in the writer, no surprise in the reader" (1972, 440). When we write from a place of gravity, when we revisit moments that filled us with curiosity, fear, annoyance, sadness, joy, humor, or pride, we are likely to convey similar feelings to our readers. And when I find myself surprised by something while I write—shocked that I suddenly remember the scent of my father's pipe tobacco—it fills me with energy and reveals the kind of details that connect writers to readers. A willingness to sift through our memories increases the chances for authentic writing and storytelling. Doing this at home in a chair on my personal computer is one thing but sharing that work with my students is another.

The first time I felt nervous about reading my work aloud was when I decided to share my essay about the fear I felt when my son was born. Nathan arrived eight weeks early, and it was touch-and-go for the first few days after his birth. I didn't write this essay until he was six years old, healthy and active. Though I set out to write about my fear and uncertainty, the tone of the essay quickly shifted. While I was writing, I was surprised by the recent image of Nathan running around the soccer field, laughing and pumping his little fist after scoring a goal. I decided the essay would start with that image—the one that would let the readers know Nathan was alive and well. Then, I could flash back to the scary stuff, giving me and the readers some comfort in knowing that it would all turn out OK. Truth be told, the essay did give me chills (and I shed some tears) while writing it. I was proud of my work, and I wanted to share it with my students as an example of a personal narrative that challenged me.

When I started to read it aloud in front of my sixth graders, I had to take a deep breath. They could sense my apprehension. I found myself reading quickly, trying to power through, but I knew that when I got to a certain line—the same line that got me while writing the piece—I might need a break. Sure enough, I did. And the class smiled when I took another breath. I made it through, albeit with a shaky voice. They all clapped and asked questions when I'd finished. That year was the first time I remember reading a pile of diverse, authentic personal narratives from my class. I now spend less time reading polished examples from authors and more time reading work from people in our school. This provides stories that hit closer to home, from people they know, and it also demonstrates that people in our community choose to write—it's something they do on their own time. It's an art form that connects us.

This experience also made me think about reading aloud fiction in class. Most of us are understanding and accepting when we have to keep a box of tissues nearby when reading aloud an emotional book written by someone else. Why do we tend to be more comfortable shedding tears when sharing someone else's work rather than ours? Why do we shy away from reading something we've written that might result in a similar emotional reaction? Because it is our own work we are revealing—it's more personal. The emotional exposure is more intense, the uncertainty and risk are elevated. But I believe that risk has big payoffs. It builds community and trust and demonstrates to students that we are walking the walk. We are in the game with our students, struggling, sharing, feeling, being human.

Personal Vulnerability in Action:
A Letter About Bullying

I'd always prided myself on establishing a strong classroom community. I believed, and still do, that the most profound learning takes place when the environment is a safe one. One year, however, my sixth-grade class became divisive; there were cliques, which led to bullying, which led to exclusion. Despite my best efforts, I could not bring this group together, and the learning suffered. Unlike my previous classes, this one was not willing to openly discuss the tensions in the room.

At a loss for what to do, I wrote them a letter (see Appendix for the letter to the class). I wrote about my own middle school experience, how I lost friends because I was concerned with my status, how, even at the time, I knew that my behavior was misguided, but I carried on regardless. I asked my students to read my letter and respond in writing. I invited them to write about what they saw happening in our class, what they might do to ease the tension. They wrote for an entire period.

When I read their papers that evening, I was shocked. Students admitted to bullying behavior, several stating that in previous years they had been bullied, and now they were the aggressors. Others explained that they wanted to stand up to the bullying but feared retribution. The next day, several students thanked me for allowing them to write. Though they weren't comfortable talking about it as a class, it felt good to share on paper. There was a new awareness, and it helped to alleviate some of the tension in the classroom. I wouldn't say that group ever became a tight-knit community, but relationships slowly improved after the letter-writing experience.

I wondered: Was it the invitation to write about bullying that helped? Or was it the fact that I shared a relevant personal story? Was it both? I can't be certain, but I've always believed that this quiet act of vulnerability helped to initiate change. If nothing else, in a classroom that was not emotionally safe for my students, the writing opportunity gave a comfortable space to share honest reflections.

Though this was a low-risk move on my part, it still required the sharing of a time in my life of which I was not proud. I vividly recall ignoring my friends in middle school, hoping to gain the attention of a cooler group. I didn't like admitting that to my class, but I felt that, to ask them to self-reflect, I needed to be honest, to share this memory and how it eventually impacted my ability to empathize.

Relational Vulnerability

Relational vulnerability encompasses *admitting fault, offering genuine apologies, listening deeply, and giving specific, heartfelt compliments.*

I can only think of one occasion in all of my years as a student when a teacher apologized to me. I was in eleventh grade, and I hated math. I had always struggled to understand concepts, to keep up with the pace of the class. This teacher liked to have students solve problems on the board in front of everyone. One day, she instructed me to solve an equation from the homework. I told her I didn't understand the problem. She held firm, and I was required to attempt to solve the problem on the board. I stood there, humiliated, staring at a string of letters and numbers without a clue. Finally, after what felt like ten minutes of silence, she told me to go back to my seat and reminded me that I needed to spend more time with the homework. I already felt like a helpless loser when it came to math, and now she confirmed it in front of everyone. I was livid.

Had this happened in elementary school, I would have likely told my parents, and they would have talked to the teacher, and the teacher would have avoided me for the rest of the school year. But I had a good relationship with my guidance counselor, who listened to my concerns and told me she would speak to the teacher and maybe then we could all talk. And we did. The three of us sat in a room and I shared how the experience made me feel about math and my self-worth. The teacher listened; she really heard me. She sighed, leaned forward, looked me in the eye, and said, "I'm sorry. I should not have asked you to come to the board. I should have offered to work with you during a free period. I hope you'll take me up on that offer now."

I remember being speechless. I was ready for her to be defensive, to blame me for my lack of studying. But when she took responsibility for being part of the problem, it made me want to do the same. At that moment, I realized that I could have been working harder. I didn't need to give up on math. I accepted her apology, told her I would try harder, and started to work with her during my free period. Things got better. I did not learn to love math, but I began to have the patience and desire to try a little harder. This only occurred because my teacher was able to demonstrate compassion and admit fault. Her ability to offer a genuine apology immediately took the wind out of my angry sails and helped me see that I, too, was part of the problem.

Somehow this experience did not immediately translate from student-David to teacher-David. I went many years as a teacher without offering a genuine apology. Several times I knew I messed up, overreacted during class, and came back the next day to apologize. In reality, my apologies were not authentic; they all included a *but*. "Hey, class. I'm sorry I raised my voice yesterday. I shouldn't have done that, *but* several of you were . . ." At the time, I thought I was sharing the blame, but really my message was this: *I wouldn't have to raise my voice if you would all just behave!* This is not an apology. So what does an authentic apology look like and why is it so difficult to give?

Harriet Lerner, psychologist and author of *Why Won't You Apologize?*, explains why offering a genuine apology is so hard:

> Apologizing means sharing vulnerability. It is vulnerable to apologize. You don't know how your apology will be received. You don't know if it will open up the floodgates to more criticism.
>
> In order to give a heartfelt apology for something really important you need to have a solid platform of self-worth to stand on and from that higher platform you can look out at your bad

> behavior and you can see it as part of a more complex ever
> changing picture of who you are as a human being. People who
> do serious harm stand on a small rickety platform of self-worth
> and they're not able to really get it. They're not able to really own
> the harm that they've done because it threatens to flip them into
> an identity of worthlessness and shame. (Safe Space Radio 2018)

If we are to offer an authentic apology, Lerner shares, we need to do the following:

> You should be sincere. You should take full responsibility for
> what you said or did or failed to say or do without a hint of obfus-
> cation or bringing up the other person's crime sheet—without
> any ifs ands and buts and that is very difficult. (Lerner 2018)

Offering a sincere apology, whether it's to an individual student or a class as a whole, is difficult. It's a rare thing in our personal lives, and I believe it's even scarcer in schools. Recently, as I've become more aware of my own tendency to be defensive, to blame others for my mistakes, I'm better able to remove myself from the experience, and ask, "What would my behavior look like to an outsider?" I try to replay the scenario in my mind with someone else playing my role. Should this guy apologize? If the answer is yes, then when I'm ready to say I'm sorry, I need to consider my tone and word choice; this will likely be the difference between a flippant, inauthentic apology and a sincere, heartfelt one.

Sincere, Specific Compliments:
Moving Beyond "Great Job!"

If offering an apology is so difficult, giving someone a compliment should be easy, right? Turns out, no. I don't think many of us are really good at giving sincere compliments; they require a similar kind of relational vulnerability. Think about the feedback that many teachers write on paper or the verbal comments offered after a presentation. These tend to focus on what's wrong with the work, what might be improved. However, even when compliments are given or strengths are pointed out, they tend to be brief and somewhat generic: "Great job!" "Well done!" "Super!" "Awesome work!"

Many teachers are overwhelmed with large class sizes, which makes it daunting to think about carefully assessing and offering meaningful feedback for over a hundred students. It's understandable that we've resorted to these quick one- or two-word compliments. However, not every draft or paper needs to be graded, and some of the best feedback can be offered verbally during a writer's workshop approach. The previous compliments do little to show the student what they did well or why their work was awesome. We tend to give more specific feedback when it's negative. It's easier to mark specific errors: run-on sentences, confusing paragraphs, and misplaced commas. It requires a shift in thinking to point out *why* a certain passage revealed such strong imagery or *how* the writer's pace and tone made us want to keep reading. But if we take the time to recognize these student successes, it will go a long way toward building relationships and reminding our students what good writing looks like. Lack of time is not the only reason teachers avoid offering quality compliments. It can make both parties uncomfortable.

Offering a sincere compliment requires vulnerability on the part of the giver. When we look someone in the eye and explain all the details of what they did well—whether it's related to their schoolwork or their behavior—it can make us feel exposed. The receiver may laugh it off, say that it was nothing. This could minimize our efforts. If we've just taken the time and emotional energy to deliver a compliment and it's met with a dismissive wave of the hand or a wrinkled brow, we may feel that our message went unappreciated. When teachers take the time to share a compliment, we hope that the student receives it well, that it sinks in and, just like an apology, is accepted.

Receiving a compliment also requires vulnerability. In my experience, students often find it even more difficult to receive a compliment than to accept an apology. Sitting in the presence of an adult at school, listening to us explain why their behavior at recess filled us with pride or why the opening paragraph of their essay brought tears to our eyes, will make even the most confident students squirm in their seats. There may be several reasons for this. If the compliment stands in stark contrast to their self-image, they may be confused, wary about what we're saying. For example, if we compliment a student on how well they articulated their thinking during a class discussion, and they believe that voicing their opinions is a personal weakness, this may create confusion; they are likely to be skeptical of the compliment, and that's where we might see the furrowed brow. It's also likely that they aren't used to hearing adults point out specific strengths in such a personal way. This lets the student know that we are really seeing them. That may create discomfort as well.

It may take some time, but when students realize that this is not a one-time thing, that the adults in the school recognize their strengths and are willing to point them out, it builds trust, confidence, and community.

It's easy to remain safe in our teaching lives, to avoid these personal encounters, interactions that are almost guaranteed to make us feel something. But like so many things in life, if fear gets in the way of doing something we feel is right, it's most likely a sign that we need to jump in. There has never been a time when I've offered an apology or a compliment and later regretted it. But there have been plenty of times when I've failed to do either and have wished that I had. When we apologize authentically and compliment sincerely, we begin to humanize our schools.

Relational Vulnerability in Action: *Cross-Generational Poetry*

For several years, I've asked my students to write "where I'm from" poems (modeled after a George Ella Lyon [n.d.] activity), which offers a snapshot of their lives. These poems require students to capture all the aspects that make them unique. It's typically a high-interest endeavor, one that elicits much sharing. One year, I decided to extend the unit. What if we shared our poems with residents in a retirement community? What if we interviewed the residents and wrote about them?

We took a field trip to a retirement home where pairs of my students sat with a resident. Each student explained our poetry project and read aloud their poems. Next, my students interviewed the residents, listening deeply and asking questions about their childhood, young adulthood, and adult lives. My students' body language, smiles, head nods, and follow-up questions showed that they were in the moment with the residents. Demonstrating this deep listening and acknowledging the residents' stories required relational vulnerability. We recorded the interviews, and after returning to school, we began drafting "where I'm from" poems about each resident. We refined our work and returned to the retirement home, where we read aloud our new creations—personal tributes to our new friends. Reading these poems—summations of each resident's life in poetry form—required relational vulnerability on the part of the reader and the listener. There were tears and long conversations. Email addresses were exchanged, and everyone promised to stay in touch. Several residents grabbed my hand—firmly yet kindly—to tell me how much this interaction meant to them. Weeks later, several residents traveled to attend our school musical. The next summer, we were invited to a reception, as the residents proudly viewed the poetry, now framed and hanging in their hallway. I've repeated this project several times, and each time, students note that it's one of their most impactful school experiences.

This project frightened me at first. I'd be taking students to meet strangers with whom they'd share some personal poetry. Was it fair of me to do this? Some of the students were resistant, because they were uncomfortable sharing too much with someone they didn't know. Their initial poems were somewhat reserved, and that was OK. They didn't need to share anything that would make them feel uncomfortable. But after our initial meeting, many revised their poems, added more personal stories, and couldn't wait to return to the retirement community to read aloud their updated drafts. The risk paid off, and the response—after the initial discomfort—was overwhelmingly positive.

When students shared their "where I'm from" poems with the residents, it opened a door. When the residents reciprocated with stories of their own, it deepened the connection. Students listened deeply to the stories and, through poetry, highlighted the specific strengths and accomplishments of their new friends. Witnessing the cross-generational collaboration and the ensuing joy was magical. Everyone took risks in sharing personal stories, and by the end, relationships were cemented. I had no doubt that my students were deeply engaged in the kind of learning that one will never forget.

Dialogic Vulnerability

Dialogic vulnerability is *inviting crucial conversations into the classroom, even if these topics might create discomfort and tension.*

I would like to apologize to all of my former students who endured the school uniform debate/persuasive writing activity, which I led for years. Debating and writing about whether or not students should wear uniforms to school was such a safe, easy debate, so I recycled it for several years. The routine went like this: I showed an image of school uniforms, pointing out the common clothing requirements for each gender. Next, I asked students who were in favor of this requirement to go to one side of the classroom, and those who were against, to go to the other side. Students who were unsure could stay in the middle. Anyone could move freely to either side (or the middle) if their opinion shifted. This was a slam dunk in terms of class participation. Most kids had an opinion on this one way or the other. After the debate, students wrote persuasive essays that basically reiterated the highlights of our discussion.

Eventually, I realized this activity lacked several key components of healthy classroom dialogue: the topic was teacher-selected, and I never asked the students what they might want to discuss or debate. It was also removed from their personal experience. Most of the students in my classes had never worn a school uniform, so we were all passing judgment on something we'd never experienced. Finally, the topic was safe; there was no urgency in the conversation, little reason to have the discussion, because it ultimately didn't impact the people in the room. Why weren't we talking about issues that impacted the students' lives? Wouldn't that have led to a richer, more meaningful conversation? Of course, but it would require vulnerability on my part. I would have to be willing to discuss topics that might make me or others in the room feel some discomfort.

Books offer endless opportunities for us to access these conversations. We've read and discussed books like *Genesis Begins Again by* Alicia D. Williams (2019), *Locomotion by* Jacqueline Woodson (2003), and *The Hate U Give* by Angie Thomas (2017). These books address themes like colorism, loss of a loved one, and police brutality. Until recently, however, I kept the conversations safe, focusing on the characters' lives rather than connecting them to what's happening in our world today. Again, I was protecting myself from dialogic vulnerability.

During my action research project with Heinemann, I started to facilitate conversations that required me to lean into discomfort. I found myself needing to read more closely and think about how the story elements connected to local and national news events. I stopped limiting the scope of our conversations and, instead, pushed all of us to move away from the characters in the book and look at the related issues in our community, our country. I will not lie; I was nervous, and there were times when I felt deeply exposed. I wondered what my principal would think if he walked in during one of our more intense conversations. I learned very quickly, however, that my students were ready; they were less afraid than I was to engage in real-world conversations. I needed to embrace my discomfort as a learning opportunity—something we ask our students to do regularly, but forget to require of ourselves as teachers.

Dialogic vulnerability requires a shifting of power. Not only do I need to allow space for students to discuss real-world topics, I need to accept that I may not be an authority on the issue at hand. In the past, the topics we've discussed and debated have been relatively safe. But my students want to talk about our school's dress code and why it targets females; they want to engage in discussions about gun violence; they need to have conversations about race and privilege. I may need to look outside my classroom and invite colleagues, parents, and community members who are more knowledgeable than I am to help facilitate some of these conversations. But when I do, I want to be a part of them; I want to allow our conversations to continue after the experts leave the classroom.

Dialogic Vulnerability in Action: *Discussing Parkland*

Another school shooting. In the past, after such tragedies, there was quiet conversation among the students, whispers of, "Did you hear what happened?" But after the mass shooting at Stoneman Douglas High School, a small group of eighth graders in our school took action. With the national walkout day forthcoming, they presented their ideas to our principal. We decided to meet in the auditorium, where volunteers read a bio of each victim. Next, interested students and staff walked outside, linked arms, and formed a circle around our school—a symbol of protection. Finally, we gathered as a whole school to reflect on the experience.

The ensuing discussion was powerful. Never have I witnessed such honesty, such a sincere sharing of worries, hopes, anger, confusion, and a fierce sense of activism. Our school is founded on student voice and shared leadership. We pride ourselves on building and maintaining a strong community. But sometimes our efforts to reach this goal feel forced. This day, however, one seventh grader stood up and said, "I know we do community-building activities every week, and they are supposed to bring us closer together. But I have never felt as close to any of you as I do today. Being able to talk about this with all of you has made our community stronger than it's ever been."

Allowing this kind of open sharing in a public school required courage on the part of our administrator. It took courage for students and staff to share so openly. Even for those who didn't speak, it invited an opportunity to demonstrate compassion for their peers who were visibly emotional. This was only possible because those in leadership positions took risks, made themselves vulnerable.

Relationships First: Now More Than Ever

When the COVID-19 pandemic hit the United States, I, like many educators, spent the last three months of the 2019–2020 school year teaching to a computer screen. Most of what I love about teaching was taken away. With no time for preparation, I needed to transition my courses to 100% online learning. I work in a privileged community, so our students all had district-issued Chromebooks. The district also made it possible for every family to have internet access. We were told to meet with each class via Zoom at least twice per week. Learning was to be asynchronous, because we could not expect students to show up at their computer at a specific time. I appreciated that our administrators took this into consideration. We couldn't know what was happening in each household; our middle schoolers might be responsible for helping to take care of younger siblings while their parents worked. As was the case for many, my class attendance was meager.

Often, students who did attend Zoom calls kept their video off. I missed them and wanted to see their faces, hoped to make them smile, and longed to laugh with them like we did in school. But even my most talkative students were reserved on Zoom. Most looked deflated, and as the year wore on, it only got worse. I often felt like I was filling time, putting on a one-man show. I was exhausted at the end of each day, and all I'd done was sit in my chair and talk to a computer screen. I did have one class that showed up in greater numbers and participated in our conversations. Every once in a while, a student would say something to make the group smile, and I would catch a few seconds of laughter and joy. These were fleeting, but I soaked them up. That's what I missed about the classroom. The human interaction, the connection, the messiness of real conversations. All of this requires three-dimensional interaction, where we can see facial expressions and read the energy in the room. The human element of teaching had been lost.

As I am writing this in the spring of 2021, I'm hopeful that we will be back in the classroom next fall. If not, I'll still be expected to deliver the curriculum, and the students will be required to complete their assignments. That element of schooling will occur no matter what. Some outside of education may feel that the important work will still be accomplished; I would disagree. Classroom and school community has always been a priority for me. But the pandemic helped many educators realize just how fundamental relationships are to everything we do in

THERE HAS NEVER BEEN A TIME WHEN I'VE OFFERED AN APOLOGY OR A COMPLIMENT AND LATER REGRETTED IT. BUT THERE HAVE BEEN PLENTY OF TIMES WHEN I'VE FAILED TO DO EITHER AND HAVE WISHED THAT I HAD.

school, work, and life. I've never liked the idea that school should be preparation for real life. School is part of real life. And no matter what stage of life we are in, building strong relationships is an essential part of what enables us to learn.

I miss my students. They miss each other. I cannot imagine coming back together and diving into the curriculum without reconnecting, talking, listening to one another's stories. Our collective relational cups are empty, and we will need to find a way to refill them.

My principal, Dr. Jon Downs, brought our staff together for a final, remote meeting at the end of the school year. Prior to the pandemic, he'd been grappling with how to balance our whole-school community-building time with instructional time. There had been tension among the staff; some were pushing for more field trips and community-building time, and others felt beholden to getting through all of the curriculum to prepare students for state testing. During that meeting, Dr. Downs spoke firmly about coming to a clear decision about the value of time spent building community and deepening human connection: "After we spent all of this time in remote learning, I realized that well-being should be our number-one priority. We saw that kids were hurting, teachers were hurting, principals were hurting. I decided that when we go back to school, we will not simply be jumping back into the curriculum; we'll be jumping into relationship building."

This kind of leadership required vulnerability. Our leaders feel pressure to prepare students for testing, and that can overshadow the importance of developing and maintaining a vibrant work environment. The pandemic brought into focus something Dr. Downs already knew in his heart: healthy, happy schools require staff and students to know one another, to listen deeply, and to be patient, supportive, and authentic.

During my career, there have been countless opportunities to walk into vulnerability, but I wonder how many times I've held back, resisted the chance to share a poem I'd written, avoided apologizing for the way I spoke to a student, or failed to initiate that crucial classroom conversation. Over the last few years, I've been more courageous, taken risks, and paid attention to how my willingness to be vulnerable affected the lives of my students. I still mess up—often—but I no longer let that inevitability prevent me from being real. And it turns out the more I embrace vulnerability, the more I show my students my authentic self, the more willing they are to do the same. And when that authenticity pervades a school environment, watch out—because engagement, passion, and memorable learning has the potential to run rampant.

LOOKING BACK LOOKING AHEAD

Consider answering these questions in a personal journal and then discussing with a colleague:

- When have you leaned into vulnerability in the classroom?
- How have these moments affected the community, your lessons, your growth as a teacher?
- Which dimension(s) of vulnerability (personal, relational, dialogic) have you experienced?
- Which dimension(s) of vulnerability (personal, relational, dialogic) do you consider personal strengths?
- Which dimension(s) of vulnerability (personal, relational, dialogic) offer areas of potential growth?
- What are some ways you might dip your toe into practicing vulnerability in the classroom?

PERSONAL VULNERABILITY

THIS IS WHO I AM

> TO SHARE YOUR OWN WEAKNESS IS TO MAKE
> YOURSELF VULNERABLE; TO MAKE YOURSELF
> VULNERABLE IS TO SHOW YOUR STRENGTH.
>
> —CRISS JAMI

Personal vulnerability is many things. Sometimes it's telling a personal story about what shaped our love of photography. It might be reading aloud fiction we wrote while in seventh grade. Or it could be testing out a new curricular project with a trusted colleague. All of these things are likely to make us feel uncertain and exposed. But if we want schools to be vibrant, safe spaces, where teachers and students lead and learn together, the risks are necessary.

During my time as a Heinemann Fellow, I asked students to (periodically) respond to survey questions. As an English teacher, I was especially interested in how sharing my stories might impact their own writing. So I asked the following question:

> WHEN YOUR TEACHER SHARES PERSONAL
> STORIES—THROUGH WRITING OR SPEAKING—
> DOES THIS AFFECT THE KIND OF STORIES
> YOU'RE WILLING TO SHARE WHEN WRITING AND
> SPEAKING? IF SO, HOW?

Many students noted that when teachers shared their stories, it created a space where they felt more comfortable sharing their own.

> Last year, my teacher shared a lot of personal experiences and how it helped her develop as a writer, which pushed me past my own worries to share my own personal experiences through my writing and show my true character. She shared a lot of her personal writing as well which helped all of us in the classroom smile and want to tell our own stories.

> It always makes me feel like I can be more vulnerable in what I'm sharing. The time this most affected me was when my teacher shared his piece about his dad. Ever since then, I feel that my writing has been more open, both in what I write about and the topics that I chose.

> When a teacher shares a personal experience with the class it makes me more comfortable to talk.

Other students noted that when teachers shared first, it helped them generate writing ideas and improved the overall quality of their work.

> I personally think that it has helped me write better, because I see more real examples of writing.

> I feel more willing to share a story if a teacher shares one first, because it makes me think of stories that I want to share.

Several students commented on how it strengthened relationships:

> Seeing a teacher be vulnerable teaches me as a student that teachers are still human and strengthens our relationships with them. It also encourages us to be vulnerable in our own writing.

> It does help me feel more comfortable and able to share more, because I know about the teacher's personal life and who they are as a person, and not just a classroom teacher, so when I'm turning in my assignment, I don't feel like I'm sharing my personal life with a stranger.

> I have more respect for vulnerable teachers, because the risk that they are taking can strengthen the bond between us.

There were clear patterns in my findings. The results showed that when teachers share their stories with students, it:

o increases student *engagement*

o *inspires* students to write

o gives students the *courage* to write honestly

o creates a more *comfortable* environment

o garners *respect* for teachers

o strengthens *student-teacher relationships*

o builds *trust*.

Writing and Risk-Taking

Witnessing a roomful of students typing or scribbling away, occasionally pausing to ponder a point or reconsider a sentence—this is English teacher bliss. Ideally, they are immersed in twenty different projects, twenty different stories where they might be revealing snippets of their lives, crafting powerful arguments for change, or sharing a passion. But how do we guide them to a place where they are writing for more than their teacher, for more than a grade?

Vulnerability needs to be defined for students, but it also needs to be demonstrated. Recently, I've pushed myself to share more openly and earlier in the school year. By October, my students knew I struggled as a middle schooler, have a passion for baking bread, and continue to battle perfectionism. I hope that the vulnerability I demonstrate will translate to more authenticity in our learning community.

At the start of our choice writing unit, we each came up with a proposal—this would allow us to share our topics and get feedback from one another. I decided that I would write about how a loss in our family helped me see a side of my father I'd never witnessed before. After I read my proposal, I could sense some discomfort. I don't know whether it was the gravity of the topic or the change in my body language while reading; either way, the tone was set, and I wasn't sure how it would affect the rest of the session.

Honestly, I didn't know what kind of topics my middle schoolers would propose. In many schools, curriculum requires teachers to complete fixed genre studies. But most real-world writing is a blend of several genres, and I think it's important to find space and time for at least one non-genre-specific piece. My students' topics were diverse and bold:

- an infographic about overcoming a nut allergy through oral immunotherapy

- a memoir about dealing with generalized anxiety

- a sports blog reflecting on a dreamlike season for a student's favorite football team

- a list of ten life lessons a student learned from watching her favorite television show

- an essay about the importance of foster care

- a TED Talk about the pros and cons of social media from a teen's perspective

- an editorial about Nike's commercial featuring Colin Kaepernick

- an "I Believe in Pride" essay focusing on a student's gender fluidity.

As students read these topic proposals aloud to the class, I noticed the intense quiet. I watched them as they listened to their peers. I saw direct eye contact, smiling, and head nodding. What I didn't see: doodling, side conversations, anyone asking to leave the room. Several students mentioned how creative or brave or unique a given project proposal was, and I realized I didn't need to move the conversation along; they were leading and supporting the process.

After the proposals were read, I heard that one line all English teachers love: "Can we please write now?" Next came the inevitable struggle to see these ambitious project ideas through to completion. I think they felt added pressure because they were writing for more than a grade. There was personal investment in their writing; the work they were doing would be a reflection of themselves: a personal battle, a strong belief, a story about who they are outside school. This shift has huge benefits in terms of motivation and engagement, but it also creates a new responsibility to self: *I want to do this, and I want to do it well because I care.*

As we neared the midpoint of the unit, I decided to read a draft of my essay aloud. I wrote about how my stoic father became emotional after a loss in our family. I was seventeen when it happened, and it was really the first time I saw him vulnerable. When I finished, there was silence—no clapping, no comments. I noticed one student release a long-held breath. I asked for feedback: "What worked for you? What could you see? What questions remain unanswered?" They named specific lines that stuck with them and made a couple suggestions for fleshing out a scene or two. And they thanked me for reading the essay.

Student sharing ensued, and, again, I was struck by the deep quiet and careful listening. After each reading, the feedback was supportive, specific, and honest. Later, I asked students to reflect on our session and whether my story impacted their engagement. What follows is a sampling of their responses:

> I appreciate you trusting all of us enough that you were able to share this piece about your dad.

> After you read it, the class didn't clap. Not clapping isn't always a bad thing, though. We were all just so absorbed in your story that we didn't want to snap back into reality. The entire classroom felt connected to you, and we felt connected to each other because we had all just listened to the same, vulnerable story that you shared.

> I think that when someone is sharing something vulnerable, it totally changes the atmosphere of the room and everyone gets way more engaged than they would if you were sharing something that's not as important to you.

I also asked students to reflect on how the experience might have impacted the sense of community in our classroom. Here's what they had to say:

> For me personally, whenever someone is reading something that I know is hard for them, I automatically give them 100% of my focus and respect. I get totally absorbed in what they're saying because I know they're giving me their trust and I give them all of my respect for that.

> Any time that anyone shares something vulnerable to you, you feel more comfortable sharing something vulnerable with them, so when everyone in our class, including you, is stepping out of their comfort zones, I feel like I could do the same because I trust everyone to be respectful.

> Everyone has been very good about respecting each other's topics they choose to write about for their projects and everyone is getting more and more comfortable with each other. It's a very nice community to be a part of.

I felt vulnerable while reading my essay. I was aware of my shaky voice, the few moments when I needed to pause. Modeling personal vulnerability leads to a more authentic classroom. I believe many of us experienced a new kind of quiet, a laser-focused listening that continued when students shared their own work. During our next class, we talked about the intense quiet that occurs when someone is being vulnerable. We tried to name it. "It's the kind of listening that leads to not clapping," said one student. "How about *quiet wonderment*?" I suggested. And that stuck. We've had some other moments of quiet wonderment, and they typically occur when someone has stepped into the spotlight and said, "Listen to my story—it may make you laugh, cry, or squirm in your seat. It might help you understand what I think about, struggle with, or hope to change. Inevitably, though, it's going to allow you to see me in a new way." And that, I believe, is authentic learning.

Writing in Front of Students

I've found that most English teachers think of themselves as readers, but fewer view themselves as writers; the prospect of writing "live" in front of students is scary. But it's so important for us to remember what it's like for our students to stare at that blank sheet of paper (or screen) and be asked to produce something on the spot. Many of us are far removed from our time in school, and we forget what that's like. But when we model this for our students, we remember—we feel it; this builds empathy and allows us to model all the mistake making, thinking, deleting, and uncertainty that is part of everyone's writing process.

Seventh-grade teacher Dana Ciciliot believes in modeling her work in front of students. The following story demonstrates her willingness to lean over the edge and show what it's like to struggle as a writer and thinker. Not only does she lean in, but she shares the very real pitfalls of success. That is, after a successful first demonstration, she became certain that she could never duplicate such a solid writing sample. She was instantly afflicted with imposter syndrome.

> On this particular day, I was determined to be brave and authentic in front of my student writers. I planned a fun, short writing activity to introduce a lesson on the purpose of pronouns and the ambiguity that can sometimes result from their use.
>
> Although I no longer remember the particular prompt I'd come up with, I can still remember my commitment to writing live, side by side with my students—my work projected for all to see. Obviously, the prompt wasn't a surprise to me, but I did make it a point not to preplan what I would write. I wanted my thinking and writing to unravel as my students watched; I wanted to show my students what I had always preached: You have to unapologetically get it down before you can get it right.
>
> Perhaps, despite my best efforts not to preplan, my subconscious had indeed been at work, for I spun a clever, humorous story from beginning to end without pause. As someone so used to finding fault in everything she writes, in this moment, I couldn't help the swelling pride, the secret pat on my back. In my mind, this writing experience was an affirmation of my

skills, which I had quickly and erroneously conflated with my identity, and soon after came the consequence: a debilitating fear that I would be unable to produce for my next group of students the caliber of work that I had just produced. And just like that, the self-conscious teacher and writer I had always known was back—with a vengeance: What will this group of students think of me as their English teacher if I cannot craft something perfect on the first try? What if what I write finally proves that I am not smart enough, witty enough, worthy enough to be their teacher?

So what did I do? I pulled out a fresh piece of paper and pushed my previous story off to the side but close enough that I could sneak glances at it and copy it almost word for word, all the while pretending the ideas were new.

It didn't take long for me to realize how damaging my decision was for both my students and me. Yet, as cringe-worthy as my decisions were, I don't regret them. After all, who among us doesn't wish we would run into our former students and apologize profusely for some of the messages we unintentionally conveyed?

What the experience taught me was to be honest.

I should have shared my worry with my second group of students. I should have normalized what it really means to be a writer, should have been willing to model what it looks like to struggle, to solve problems, to forgive, to move on, to realize that no piece of writing is indicative of who I am.

When we are vulnerable enough to take risks and make mistakes in front of our students, we (as adults students look up to) unmask what it means to be human—and brave, empathetic, evolving humans at that.

I realize that not only have I become less critical of myself by practicing vulnerability in some aspects of my class but also less critical of my students. Although I never intended to be overly critical of them, I realize the way we treat ourselves will undoubtedly extend to the way we treat others.

> It was reading about and hearing stories from other teachers writing in front of their students that motivated me to muster the courage to do the same. Perhaps the more we reflect and share our stories and what we've learned from them, the more we can not only encourage teacher vulnerability in schools but also help to support each other as we commit to this brave endeavor.

This story embodies what it means to be a vulnerable teacher. Dana did not have to write in front of her students. It was not a curricular requirement, and it would have been far easier for her to write, revise, and edit something ahead of time. But that would not have demonstrated the painfully difficult—and surprisingly rewarding—act of writing. By leaning into discomfort, Dana made her students feel more at ease in the classroom.

How It Impacts Students

One of the many benefits of teacher vulnerability is the likelihood of students joining us for the ride. When we, as teachers, openly show students who we are, they often want to do the same. It was no coincidence that after I shared the essay about my father, many students wrote about topics that were close to their hearts. It's important to note that we are not rewarding the disclosure of deeply personal information or stories. I always emphasize that each of us has the right to write about what moves us. If it's a soccer team, great! If it's exploring a favorite food, fantastic! If it's writing about a personal struggle, we welcome it! I assure students that they will not be forced to share with the class, and that if it's something they would rather not make public, I'd be the only one reading it. I'm less interested in the topic they choose and more interested in their reason for choosing it.

Since becoming a more vulnerable teacher, I've noticed that small talk in my classroom has all but disappeared. Vulnerability repels superficiality. We talk about what matters to us, what makes us laugh, what we wonder about, and what drives us to explore. Seventh-grade student Maya is an example of someone who began to see the power of personal vulnerability. After witnessing several of her teachers take emotional risks, she decided to dive in.

Sharing about my anxiety and OCD [obsessive-compulsive disorder] is always hard for me. I know that there is a lot of stigma around mental health, and that a lot of people think having OCD is just being tidy and obsessively neat. When I hear people say things like "I am so OCD about this," it hurts. But I know that they are not doing it out of hate, they are doing it out of ignorance.

I have shared about my OCD in a few different essays, but every time it is still hard. I know that there is a risk of judgement, and that mental health is just not talked about a lot. So each time I write about my own mental health experiences, I tend to delete it, then think better of it and rewrite it, sometimes multiple times. I worry about whether people will understand it, or whether it is actually relevant to the piece or not. But it always is relevant, because it is a part of who I am. Just not a part people often share about. Watching people read those things that I wrote always makes me nervous in a different kind of way, but it always turns out okay.

I continue to include mental health in some of the things I write because of the stigma and ignorance surrounding the topic. By not sharing about it, I am not helping the issue. If I can help educate people, even just a little bit, then it is worthwhile. It also makes me feel good after I share it with people. It makes me feel like I accomplished something, and that I was authentic with my writing. It is nerve wracking, but at the same time I feel successful, and that people know me better. It takes a lot of vulnerability for me to write about my mental health, but sharing about mental health needs to be normalized.

Working to destigmatize mental health issues is not something most middle schoolers would choose to tackle. However, because Maya feels safe in her learning environment, and because her teachers have welcomed authentic topics, she feels empowered to explore how her words might help others see the issue in a new light. I wonder, if we welcomed this kind of writing and thinking from the first days of kindergarten, what would our schools look like?

Writing is magical in so many ways. I am in awe of its ability to nurture personal and academic growth in both loud and quiet ways. Some students are comfortable sharing their stories through conversation—boldly stating their experiences and points of view—but others may be more at ease with vulnerability in their writing. Tenth grader Miranda reflects on her middle school experience, where she felt encouraged to be her authentic self.

> I am most comfortable being vulnerable in my writing. I fell in love with creative writing in middle school, and felt like it was the time where I could be most authentically myself. I had incredible teachers who were vulnerable and encouraged vulnerability inside the classroom. I remember once having an assignment where I wrote about my mom. I embedded our relationship into a fictional short story, but it was still my mom. We anonymously passed our stories around the room and left comments on each other's writing. No one knew I wrote it, and no one knew who it was about, but the notes I received made me feel safe sharing my stories in the class. And I wasn't the only one being vulnerable, we were each offering a small piece of ourselves up for judgement. It didn't matter that the pieces were anonymous, we had created a space in which it was safe to share our thoughts.

Invitation and Action Steps:
Write in Front of Your Students

Plan to write in front of your students. This is not the same as sharing your writing with them. Certainly, there is a time and place to share previously written examples of your work, but thinking aloud through the writing process in front of the class will demonstrate an authentic struggle to compose. You will undoubtedly delete words, change your mind, misspell, and surprise yourself with the occasional strong sentence. The students will see it all. And they will benefit, because the process is real, the struggle is real, and they will know—because you've demonstrated it—that writing rarely comes out right the first time.

I recommend starting out with lower-stakes "live writing." I often use quick writes with my students (I highly recommend Linda Rief's [2018] *The Quick-write Handbook* as a resource). I display an image or a quote and ask students to write for three to four minutes without stopping. I remind them not to worry about spelling and punctuation when completing a quick write. The purpose is to generate ideas that might be used for larger projects down the road. Modeling a quick write in front of students is a good way to ease into this activity. Students may see you struggle to come up with ideas, jump from topic to topic, and make faces as you write. Try it out. Here's a quick write prompt that's sure to generate a memorable classroom writing experience:

> WRITE ABOUT YOUR FAVORITE (OR LEAST FAVORITE) COLOR. WHAT IS THE FIRST THING THAT COMES TO MIND WHEN YOU THINK OF THIS COLOR. WHAT MEMORIES, OBJECTS, SENSES, WORDS, FEELINGS ARE ASSOCIATED WITH IT?

Sharing Personal Stories

How much of our life outside of school should we share with students? What mistakes should remain hidden from our conversations? Answers to these questions depend on our intention behind the sharing and the experiences of the students in front of us, and of course we all need to know our boundaries. We should never blindside students with personal stories for the sake of being vulnerable. Doing this may come off as self-serving, and out-of-the-blue oversharing is never OK. We should not put the burden of being compassionate on our students; rather, our sharing should be purposeful and intentional.

High school teacher Kate Walker was excited to apply for a summer literary seminar for teachers. Part of the application process required Kate to write a personal essay. At the same time, she was guiding her students through the college essay process; she thought it would be an ideal time to share her work with students.

> Every year, I would take my seniors through the process of writing college essays, although for me, I just applied to the public

college that was closest to me in Connecticut, so I often struggled to understand just what they were feeling as they wrote these essays that they placed so much importance on what fueled them.

In 2018, I discovered there would be an NEH [National Endowment for the Humanities] summer seminar on *Moby Dick*, and so I realized as I began to shape my essay for entry into this experience that I was essentially doing the same thing my seniors were, at the same time. I decided to share my process of writing an essay for the summer seminar. We went through it together, and I shared stories about my personal life through the narrative process—what it was to grow up in New England, surrounded by stories of whaling, pirates, and *Moby Dick*. How much that book had influenced my life in college, and in personal trips to the Whaling Museum in New Bedford— and what it would mean to be able to go and study with other *Moby Dick* nerds for two weeks in the summer.

I projected my essay up on the board, and as a class, we talked through it. I had to explain that part of summers growing up involved going to Cape Cod, playing on the beach, and pretending to see Moby Dick in the waves—and I didn't think that part should be cut out, even though students thought it was unnecessary. I found myself making similar arguments my own students had—but that is an important part of the story! And realizing that students were right when they suggested I cut it, because it was less important than the work I did in my classroom.

Students suggested I should smooth out portions, clarify other parts, and work on more active verb choice. Although I often write while my students are writing, this was the first time I cared about an essay in a similar way that they did to their college essays. If I didn't get into the seminar, I would be upset.

When I was deferred entrance to the seminar, students shared my sadness, and when I was finally admitted, they shared my success. This process of making myself vulnerable and talking through the changes I made to my application

> essay not only made me a better teacher for my students, but it demonstrated to my students that even I struggled to write and revise, and I needed to work through what I wanted to say, what my message was, and how I should convey that. I believe that process made sharing writing that year easier for students because they saw me put myself out there and realized it would help them become better writers to share their work.

Kate took a personal risk in sharing her story. She had valid reasons for writing and revising alongside her students. She demonstrated that she, too, is a writer who struggles, fails, rewrites, and needs advice. Her willingness to share her writing process and connect that sharing to their work in school enabled students to see her as a real, three-dimensional person. This is an excellent example of how an intentional risk of personal vulnerability can simultaneously strengthen relationships and increase engagement

How It Impacts Students

When I asked seventh grader Nikola if they could share a memory related to personal vulnerability, they explained the difference between *planned* and *in-the-moment* vulnerability, offering an example of each:

> For me, there are two main types of vulnerability: planned vulnerability and in-the-moment vulnerability. Planned vulnerability is the vulnerability you think about before sharing. It could be anything from an English project you've spent a while on to a contribution to a discussion that you think about for a few minutes. In-the-moment vulnerability is the vulnerability that just comes out of you when you don't expect it. For me, it is often in incredibly emotional times and can be just as meaningful as planned vulnerability.
>
> One of the most valuable experiences of planned vulnerability for me was when I shared my memoir, "I Believe in Pride." I had worked on that memoir for 3 months, and I was proud of what I had created. I was aware that sharing it would

be vulnerable, but I had no way of gauging how vulnerable it would be until I shared it. When I shared it, I felt nothing too special about it until it was over. I have always been comfortable with my identity, and I have no fear of letting people know about it. But in the end, when I was able to see people's reactions, I realized that I just did something brave. It was odd being the person who was affecting others. I have been so inspired by vulnerability whenever I've seen it from others, and it was (and still is) amazing to think that I could have done even a sliver of that for the people who heard me share and be vulnerable.

In-the-moment vulnerability is a much more interesting type of vulnerability to me. One of the most memorable experiences of it was the discussion after the school walk-out that I participated in to protest gun violence. The walk-out itself felt powerful to me, and there was a type of unspoken vulnerability to it. But, for me, the discussion afterward was the most powerful part.

Everyone taking part in that discussion was vulnerable in their own ways. The whole experience of it was truly breathtaking. When I stood up to speak, I had next-to-no idea of what to say. I just followed my emotions and was vulnerable. There was no planning, no preparation. But, that experience for me was just as powerful as that essay I had spent months preparing. For the rest of the people in that discussion, I doubt my contribution changed much. But, the whole effect of everyone being vulnerable was impactful for everyone.

I had never thought about this distinction until Nikola shared their perspective. Almost all of my vulnerability had been planned and intentional. The in-the-moment kind is a much scarier proposition; it puts me in the moment, and for someone who likes to consider their risks before taking them, I'm much less likely to lean into vulnerability in the moment. Still, Nikola has clearly found a worthwhile distinction and one that should be considered when discussing vulnerability in school.

Students often recognize school hierarchies. Teachers are in charge of students, principals are in charge of teachers, and people students rarely see are in charge of principals. Eleventh grader Margo recognized the power of teacher vulnerability as a means to break down these traditional hierarchies:

> Often as a student, I feel as if teachers are at a higher level than me, that they see themselves above me and my peers. But with teachers being open about their pasts, their futures, and willingness to own up to their mistakes, as a student I feel as though I can connect with those who are guiding me to my future. One of the best ways to learn is to hear first-hand experiences of mistakes, growth, downfalls, and optimistic futures. Without vulnerability, knowledge often feels purposeless, as though due to a lack of personal experience, it cannot be real. But when an environment features stories and experiences of the past and the present, education becomes whole.

I love Margo's observation: "Without vulnerability, knowledge often feels purposeless, as though due to a lack of personal experience, it cannot be real." There is tremendous power in telling our stories. When we share our experiences, struggles, and successes, we are modeling authenticity and good storytelling, and we are organically building community. But we are also deepening relationships, letting students know that we are fallible, and carving out a space where we can be honest and talk about what matters.

Invitation and Action Steps: *Write and Share a Personal Story*

It's OK to write this one ahead of time. In fact, it's probably best to do so. When I shared a memoir about my son being born prematurely, I wanted to convey the love I instantly felt, followed quickly by fear of the unknown, and ultimately the joy in knowing he was going to be OK. If the story had a not-so-happy ending, I would not have shared it. That kind of story would have crossed my boundaries, and frankly, it would likely have been too much for my students. If we know of students who have experienced trauma, we must take that into consideration when deciding what and how much to share. If possible, prepare students ahead of time; let them know that in a week, you'll be sharing a story about _____. If they feel it will be too much, give them the option of sitting that one out. Even if we are willing to share something that is painful, we should always consider the impact it may have on students. It's not OK to put too much on them; this requires us knowing our students well, understanding what each community is ready to hear and discuss. That will change from year to year, from period to period. Use the following ideas to explore possible story topics.

- Set a timer for five minutes and write continuously about your strongest memories. Don't limit yourself; just write everything that comes to mind.

- Read your list of memories. Circle a few that stand out as possible topics to share with your students.

- Walk away from your list and come back in a few hours or the next day. Revisit your list and choose the topic that feels right for you and your students.

- Begin writing about your topic. Dive into the little moments and spend time writing about the sensory details. Remember to slow the action down when you get to the crucial moments.

- Read your piece aloud in front of the mirror or to a family member. When you think it's ready, read it to a colleague and ask them to listen as if they were a student. Ask for feedback: "Was it too much? Did I overshare? Were there passages I should cut? What stood out/made you feel something? What questions do you have for me?"

Giving the Gift of Writing

Middle school teacher Paul McCormick offers a class called "The Pursuit of Happiness." In this course, students write a gratitude letter to someone they respect and value in their life—an exercise created by the father of positive psychology, Dr. Martin Seligman. The writer is to name concrete reasons why they are grateful for this person. After writing the letter, they are challenged to read it to the recipient. The recipient may not interrupt; they need to listen to the letter in its entirety before reacting. Paul knew that if he were going to ask his students to do this, he needed to dive in as well. He wrote a letter to his father and had a difficult time reading it aloud to his class.

> I remember seconds before I was about to read it to the class, I was thinking, this is really weird, this is strange because I'm not sure this is what they (students) expect a teacher to do. As soon as I started reading it, you could hear a pin drop. The room got absolutely quiet. There is a quiet that falls over the room. They are watching me. They are like, I am seeing Paul in a new way. I am seeing Paul at an emotional edge. He's not my teacher, he is a person. He is a human being who is feeling something right now. It evokes something in other students to say I know what you're talking about. I have had that emotional feeling myself. This makes me think of a book by Sonia Nieto called *Why We Teach*. There's a quote in there that says, we don't teach what we know, we teach who we are. If you're not telling kids who you are, if you're hiding who you are as a teacher, there's some sort of barrier between you and your kids.

After Paul shared his letter with students, they began thinking about who their own recipients might be. I happened to be in the hall as they spread out in groups and shared their thinking with one another.

The energy was palpable, and from the wild hand gestures and biting of nails, it was easy to see just how nervous students were about the assignment. Still, there was excitement around this very real and vulnerable project. So often in school students complete their work for the teacher's eyes only, but here Paul was asking them to write and present to a friend or family member. And the letter needed to be written from the heart. Initially, it made people uncomfortable. The prospect of writing the letter was tough, and many students couldn't imagine reading it aloud. That kind of vulnerability just wasn't something that was part of their practice. But as the stories of reading to parents, grandparents, siblings, and friends began pouring in, it was clear that this was an impactful assignment that would not be forgotten.

When I spoke with Paul about this assignment, he shared his thinking and intention behind the project:

> The way I set it up, in my mind, was to think about how I can get kids to go somewhere a bit deeper (emotionally) with what they write, and what they experience with others. While this is entirely their choosing, ultimately, I wanted to show them that being vulnerable about my own gratitude for others is something a teacher can do in front of them—it can be modeled and exhibited in my practice. And that that can occur in school—there are no rules saying that teachers and students can't experience emotions together (or share them).

I do think that many of us are resistant to projects that might result in students and staff experiencing emotions together. But Paul is correct in stating that there are no rules against it. It's another example of how leaning into discomfort can help all of us grow as learners, thinkers, and more compassionate human beings.

How It Impacts Students

Lorelai is now a freshman in high school. She completed Paul's gratitude letter when she was in seventh grade. Looking back on the project now, it's clear that it made an impact.

> I decided to write a letter to the first friend I met in middle school. He had moved on to high school, so I missed him. I don't remember much about actually writing the letter, but I do remember being very nervous when reading it aloud. Part way through I started giggling, and it felt so awkward. I had to pause for a minute and take a deep breath. My friend was super generous and sweet in his reaction; he helped me calm down. Our teacher asked us to write a reflection afterward.
>
> Here's a bit of what I wrote [reading from her reflection]: I loved doing this assignment because it felt great telling someone how much they mean to me and how much I appreciate them. I feel like this is something I would do on my own

now. People are naturally very negative, so when they hear something super sweet or nice read about themselves, they push it away, but it's just what they need to hear.

Even two years after completing the assignment, Lorelai still squirmed in her seat while revisiting the memories of the project. It was clearly a vulnerable experience for her but one that made a big impact. At the end of our conversation, she considered pitching the gratitude letter assignment to some of her high school teachers: "I just think that would be a really nice assignment to do again."

Invitation and Action Steps: *Give a Gift of Writing*

In her book *Lessons that Change Writers*, Nancie Atwell (2017) shares a writing project called Gifts of Writing. She explains that the best gift a person can receive is a heartfelt note from a loved one. Students are encouraged to write a poem, a letter, or other form of writing that can be given as a gift. When my own daughter was in middle school, she presented her mother with a gift of writing; witnessing her read it aloud was a beautiful and unforgettable moment in our family (see Appendix for the complete letter).

Consider those in your life who have made a positive impact on your development—a relative, a friend, a colleague. It's helpful if this person is someone you can get in touch with, either in person or remotely, because you'll need to schedule a time to read your work in front of them. Create a gift of writing for that person. Here are some possibilities:

○ A gratitude letter stating specific behaviors or conversations that made an impact on you. The letter should explain how these behaviors or conversations shifted your thinking or changed you in some way.

○ A poem or series of poems that capture this person's contributions to your life.

○ A brief memoir that reflects on specific moments with this person.

Whatever form your gift of writing takes, you should be prepared to read it to the recipient. Schedule a time to share it with them and ask them not to interrupt you while you are reading. After completing the process, you'll be better prepared to lead your students through the process. And you will have an authentic example to share with them in class.

Taking a Curriculum Risk

THE DANGERS OF LIFE ARE INFINITE, AND AMONG THEM IS SAFETY.

—GOETHE

It is not necessary—nor is it advised—to disregard your current curriculum in favor of today's impulse. But there are ways to meet your required standards by choosing new and relevant material. If you are leading a unit on persuasive writing, for example, you need not use the same article from last school year. Though it may have been just what last year's group needed, there is probably something more current and motivating for the kids in front of you today. We may find it comforting to know that something has worked in the past; we might use this as our reasoning for continuing to bludgeon our students with the same lesson, year after year. Your risk might be as simple as letting go of tired resources and bringing in some fresh material. Or if you are already one who updates material every year, consider implementing a new unit that aligns with district and state standards.

Some school administrators expect a strict adherence to curriculum. Submitting lesson plans for the upcoming week is required. Standards and objectives are to be written on the board prior to each lesson. Ostensibly, these rules and practices allow for a streamlined, consistent curriculum. In reality, it doesn't necessarily result in the same content being taught across the school. Although it may feel comforting for some leaders to have everyone "on the same page," each teacher will undoubtedly bring their own style, tone, delivery method, and expectations to the classroom. They will take the curriculum and use what they know and believe to shape their lessons and delivery. As long as human beings are teaching students, no two classrooms will look alike.

Knowing this, why do we continue to resist teacher autonomy and creativity? Even in school districts that are given a fair amount of freedom, there remains an unspoken pressure to be on the same page as our colleagues. I remember teaching sixth grade; we had just adopted a new social studies unit that used a textbook as one of our resources. Lunchtime discussion seemed to always include an informal check-in with one another about what chapter we were on. Those who were behind looked visibly shaken and made comments like, "I need to move things along or I'll never catch up." No one was policing our pace or checking our lesson plans, but we seemed to be doing it to one another. This was problematic.

It's difficult to be different as a teacher. When we veer off course by developing a new unit, try out a project or assignment that's never been used at our school, we may feel vulnerable. It's risky, because we are opening ourselves up to the possibility of failure in front of our peers. Creativity expert and author Ronald A. Beghetto writes, "Creativity is risky because it requires doing things differently. And whenever we try to do something new or different, we make ourselves vulnerable to making mistakes, appearing foolish, and even being ridiculed. Put simply, creative endeavors don't always work out" (Beghetto 2018).

As a teacher who's always looking for new and creative ways to engage students, I've often felt like an outsider in school. I've never thought of myself as a rule breaker; I've argued that I'm meeting the same standards but doing so in different ways, depending on the unique needs of the students in my classroom at this moment in time. As Beghetto explains, "Classroom creativity, therefore, involves providing students with an opportunity to meet predetermined criteria in different and unexpected ways. It also requires openness to difference." I like that message: *meeting predetermined criteria in different and unexpected ways*. This is where we can do a little risk-taking and lean into our personal vulnerability when it comes to making curricular choices.

Teachers frequently encourage students to be themselves, to not try to be like everyone else. I think we could benefit from heeding our own advice, as we often feel beholden to the delivery methods and structures placed in front of us. We can find alternative, creative, and engaging ways to meet standards. It will require personal risk, and those who dive in may, at times, feel ostracized, but the potential payoff is huge. We can blame the system, the standards, the testing, but change often occurs from the bottom up, and we cannot afford to wait. Let's keep working on removing structural barriers to creativity, but while we do so, let's also push through our personal fear of failure, of retribution, of being different. "Although educators face many constraints when it comes to fostering student creativity in the classroom, the greatest barrier to creativity isn't the constraints. There will always be constraints. The greatest barrier is often ourselves and our timidity about exploring new territory. The key is to have the courage to take the beautiful risks necessary for supporting our students' (and our own) creativity" (Beghetto 2018).

My first real curriculum risk came when teaching fifth grade. I was young and had only been teaching for five years. I read an article about a teacher who took her students to a local restaurant where they were schooled in all aspects of running the business. After studying the operation, students cooked for and served their parents for an evening. I thought this was amazing and wanted to tackle something similar. As it turned out, our high school had a culinary arts program, so I contacted the chef. She was on board, and after getting permission from my administrator, we started collaborating.

Throughout the school year, my class made several trips to the high school where we were trained (by the chef and several juniors and seniors) on how to purchase ingredients, use the equipment, take orders in the cafe, and clean up. On Fridays in class, we carved out a bit of time to practice setting tables, serving, and doing the math involved. Students applied for specific roles in the restaurant and several staff members conducted interviews. We asked the parent-teacher organization for funds to purchase ingredients for an end-of-year meal, where we would prep, cook for, serve, and clean up after the students' parents, siblings, and grandparents. All profits would be donated to the Red Cross.

By May, we were ready to go. We experienced true engagement, and not just the night of the meal—I felt it throughout the entire school year. Working toward something as exciting and real as running a restaurant brought us together, and there was a layer of authenticity that permeated all of our work. When the night arrived, I was nervous. What made me think it was OK to use instructional time to teach my fifth graders how to prepare a meal? When things got rolling, there were mistakes. A couple drinks were spilled, a meal was dropped, and there was bickering among my student cooks. But it was all real, and they were learning so many valuable lessons.

Looking back on that year, I wondered what was left out of the curriculum because of our project. Not much. Occasionally, we used time on Friday afternoons for field trips and prepping for the big night. And we found ways to squeeze it into our schedule. If we finished a lesson or unit early, I didn't need to find a time filler; we already had this common goal, a project that was always on our minds. But somehow we were still able to cover the required standards.

Even though I had the backing of my principal, I didn't receive the same support from all of my colleagues. They asked things like, "How are you going to do this and still teach everything? What, are you just dropping social studies so you can have them cook for their parents?" I remember one teacher asking me to stop because it wasn't fair to her students that only mine got the chance to participate in the project.

Tackling this project required personal vulnerability. Anytime we move away from the norm, we should brace for the ensuing scrutiny. I knew that what I was doing rubbed some of my colleagues the wrong way. I opened myself up to questioning from my administrator and the parents of my students; they would all want to know how I was going to manage this and still teach the required curriculum. I won't lie, I felt uncertain and emotionally exposed until the event was over. But looking back, it was one of the most rewarding endeavors of my teaching career.

Middle school theatre teacher and colleague Leah Mueller believes that welcoming student voice is critical. Leah listens to what students need and adjusts her instruction based on these needs, which, in turn, opens the door for meaningful learning and personal growth. Here, she explains how students pushed her to take curricular risks, and she says the payoffs were huge:

> The students asked me for a ukulele ensemble. I had never played ukulele, but it kept coming up. I decided to give it a go! I found a workbook to start with "Uke Can Do It 2," which methodically got the students through note names, plucking, some chords, and a few short songs. From there we chose songs that we wanted to learn together and if we ran into a chord we didn't know—we figured it out as a class.
>
> The first semester I taught the class, I admitted to the students that I was learning too. We were all in this together. I was definitely building the plane as it was flying! Sometimes I would just be a few pages in front of the kids when I was teaching lessons. I learned that it was OK. Admitting to the students that we were all learning (including me!) was beautiful. We all leaned on each other. If one student figured out an easier way to build a chord, they would share it with the class. I saw that the students stepped up more to help each other as they felt empowered. There were some licks that the students could play better than me and they loved to show it off.
>
> Instead of me being the deliverer of knowledge, we were all on a walk together, helping each other grow. I got to see the students take ownership of their own learning. I was out of the

> classroom one day and left the guest teacher instructions that the students would run their rehearsal. It is often difficult to get a teacher who is familiar with music instruction and I felt like the students could run things on their own. A colleague shared that he looked into the auditorium and the students did an amazing job counting themselves in and playing through their pieces for the upcoming concert. That is when I feel that I have really made it as a teacher when I can step away and the students can apply what they've learned.

It's no wonder that Leah is a beloved teacher in her school. She doesn't just tell the students how important they are; she demonstrates it through listening, collaborating, and taking risks. By understanding the needs of each student and then adapting or creating lessons, units, and classes that meet them where they are, Leah is centering the students as respected members of the community. Doing so required her to be vulnerable. Personal vulnerability sometimes allows teachers to know their students deeply, which then informs their curricular decisions.

Invitation and Action Steps: *Take a Curricular Risk*

After getting to know your students, take what you've learned and consider adapting a lesson or unit to better meet their needs. How might your informational writing unit change as a result of the students in front of you this year? After understanding the interests and needs of your class, what read-alouds, novel studies, or articles might you bring in to inspire this unique group of students? Collaborate with a trusted colleague to codesign and possibly co-teach a new unit.

Open your journal to a fresh page. Spend five minutes writing about your most memorable learning experiences in school. What made them stick? What inspired you as a learner? What did the teacher do to make this experience so important? What tasks or projects were involved? Next, consider your current curriculum. Restart your five-minute timer and write about how you might adapt the current curriculum to include projects like the ones you remember. List these ideas at the bottom of your page. Run them by a trusted colleague, administrator, or curriculum specialist. Start the process of bringing these ideas to life. Repeat this process with your students. Ask them to revisit impactful learning experiences and invent new project ideas; this could lead to meaningful curricular change.

Under the right conditions, vulnerability will lead to quiet wonderment, a respectful nudge into discomfort, and a deeper sense of meaning in your classroom. By taking risks within boundaries, you are showing your students that you want school to be more than checkboxes, more than a scripted curriculum, and by joining you, they will venture into a new kind of school—the kind that leads to messy, flexible, student-driven, collaborative, and authentic learning. That's a place where they will want to learn. That's where I want to teach.

LOOKING BACK   LOOKING AHEAD

Consider answering these questions in a personal journal and then discussing with a colleague:

- Reflect on a time when you shared a memorable moment with your students. Why did you choose to share, and what were the outcomes of that experience?

- Have you ever shared your writing with your students? If so, why did you choose to do this, and how was it received?

- Would you consider composing a piece of writing in front of your students? What fears, worries, or questions do you have about doing so?

- Have you ever given someone a gift of writing? If so, is it something you might consider sharing with your students as an example?

- What curriculum risks have you taken as a teacher? In what ways have these risks helped you grow as an educator?

- What curriculum risks are percolating now? Who might be open to hearing more about these ideas?

RELATIONAL
VULNERABILITY

I'M LISTENING,
I'M SORRY,
I HEAR YOU

As teachers, we are constantly being asked to make decisions about the well-being of our students. If a student routinely asks to go to the bathroom or nurse, are they just trying to get out of class? When a student explains that they need an extra day to study for the test because of a family matter, do we make an accommodation? As we build trust and get to know our students better, these decisions become less difficult; in classrooms that embrace relational vulnerability, teachers and students know one another and are better able to communicate. This may help teachers understand underlying barriers to learning. What do relational acts of vulnerability look like from a student perspective? Here, Nina shares a memory from sixth grade when she was new to middle school and had recently lost a pet.

I hadn't any previous teachers that I felt comfortable sharing my personal life with. I vividly remember the fall of 6th grade losing my first pet ever. I had never experienced any type of loss before. I had my first class of the day with Virginia and I was supposed to present for the class. Before class had started, I went down to her office to ask if I could present the following day because the only thing on my mind was my guinea pig that had passed. I remember not expecting her to let me have an extension. When I told her the situation I was shaking tremendously and crying helplessly. In response, I received a hug from her. She went on to tell me a story about her llama she lost and showed me pictures. Not only did she give me an extension but she made me feel like I wasn't alone just by sharing a little bit of her personal life with me. I think our relationship is so special because I saw her as someone I can trust. She was able to be vulnerable with me which made me feel like I could share my struggles and joys.

Now in high school, Nina still remembers the details of this experience. It's clear that Virginia's flexibility, empathy, and care served as a foundation for the rest of their time together in middle school. Learning together becomes so much easier when a teacher demonstrates their willingness to listen and understand.

Teacher Flexibility and Empathy

Near the end of the school year, I asked my students to respond, in writing, to questions about relational vulnerability. Initially, I wanted to frame the questions in first person, so that I could learn what *I* should be doing more or less of, but for the purposes of my research, I wanted to get more global feedback about teachers in general. Following are the questions with a sampling of student responses.

WHAT HAVE TEACHERS *SAID*
THAT HELPED YOU
AS A STUDENT/PERSON?

Something that also helps my relationship with teachers is being able to just have a regular conversation with them, and having a teacher to talk to and it doesn't feel weird.

When teachers give positive feedback more than negative feedback, because it just helps to hear when you are doing something good rather than when you are just doing things that are bad.

WHAT HAVE TEACHERS *DONE*
THAT HELPED YOU
AS A STUDENT/PERSON?

When teachers are understanding of my busy schedule it also helps me. It can be stressful to try to fit everything in sometimes, and when I've been having a particularly eventful week and they understand, it really helps my mental health.

For me, whenever a teacher is just there to listen, it really helps. Whether I am ranting about random things or needing help on a project, a listening ear always does good. For me, just knowing that someone is there is really amazing.

WHAT HAVE TEACHERS *SAID*
THAT THEY
SHOULDN'T SAY AGAIN?

I really believe that the worst thing that teachers can say is nothing. It's human nature to want answers, and when you don't get any, you're often left with a feeling of being unfulfilled.

> Whenever a teacher just gives straight up criticism of a project, as in saying "This needs a lot of work," without giving any specific things I could improve on, I often find that really hard.

WHAT HAVE TEACHERS *DONE* THAT THEY *SHOULDN'T* DO AGAIN?

> Teachers need to have more mercy and forgiveness. I think that teachers just need to give students a chance to say their part sometimes.

> I really just take general inattentiveness really hard. If a teacher just doesn't pay attention to my project, I take it as them just getting bored by it and not liking it at all. That always crushed my engagement in that project, and I became much less invested in working on it.

I expected more comments about curriculum, instruction, grades, and teaching style. But most of the students' comments were about relationships, the connection or lack thereof between teacher and student. Relational vulnerability isn't a once-and-done practice. We need to be deliberate about making time to listen and know our students. In his book *Not Light, but Fire*, Matthew Kay (2018) discusses the necessity of building relationships:

> If all of our nonacademic conversations with students happen in "garbage time," or not at all, it is understandably healthy of them to maintain thick walls around their vulnerability.

> It is understandably healthy of them to trust only those who
> consider them a priority. It is understandably healthy of them
> to distrust teachers who walk them through hot button racial
> land mines, but don't know about their dance recital or new
> business, or if they won their football game. We may not always
> be invited to engage in house talk, but our odds increase once
> we create an environment of humility and genuine interest in
> one another's lives and passions. (37)

Our students want to be heard; they need us to recognize them where they are right now, as beautiful, flawed, complex individuals. They need us to be patient when they make mistakes. And most importantly, they are screaming for us to see and hear them.

Listening Deeply to Inform Practice

It was a Friday afternoon in early June. I'd just completed my twenty-first year of teaching, and I was on my way to have a drink with my eleventh-grade English teacher, who—over the years—has become a running partner and a good friend. As I approached his booth, I saw him reading. He's always early, and he's always reading. He takes a book to sporting events, and when there's a break in the action, he reads. When he's alone in a restaurant, waiting for his former student to arrive, he reads. Earlier in the day, he taught his final lesson. Freshly retired, he was a picture of contentment: his braided, gray hair rested against a black vest. He sported a burgundy fedora, and his reading glasses hung from a rainbow-colored lanyard. He smiled as I approached.

There is no small talk with Michael. He wanted to know how my year ended, if I was overly stressed, if I'd been a reflective teacher that school year. I wanted to know what it was like for him now—for someone who had dedicated his life to the profession to know it's suddenly over. I wanted him to be satisfied but sad. That would mean he'd had his bellyful of teaching but he'd miss what I'd be continuing to do for the foreseeable future. I was just about to ask, when he dove into one of his deep reflections.

"I spent the first ten years of my career trying to convince students that I was smart, that I mattered. Eventually, I learned that I should have been making the students understand that they mattered." He paused here to make the lesson more personal. "Your teaching is only going to get better, David. You're at the point in your career where you know that what really matters—more than any curriculum—is the way you look every student in the eye and listen deeply. The kind of exhausting, intense listening that shows them that they have every ounce of your attention. When you give them twenty seconds of focused listening, to the point where you are not aware of yourself, only them, the student will think 'I matter.' This is when the teaching and learning starts."

Michael's message is what I want to hold on to every day, and it's the heart of teacher vulnerability. It was inspiring to hear someone with his wisdom affirm my beliefs about the importance of relational vulnerability. And here, Michael and I are not alone. Educator and speaker Cornelius Minor (2019) writes, "There are many attributes that make someone the kind of person that kids habitually choose to learn from. When personality is fatigued, and warmth dims, or patience subsides, kids will regularly choose to invest in us if we always help them to see that what we are offering will help them to live better—in the future, of course, but most urgently, right now. The way that we get there is by listening" (15). This message reminds us that kids, far more often than adults, live in the moment, and the way to join them—right here, right now, in this moment—is to listen deeply.

Before Michael and I parted ways, he left me with one more gem: "It really doesn't matter if you're talking about a relation-ship with a friend, a student, or a family member; the purest manifestation of love is when you're listening so closely, you are only aware of the person in front of you."

After I left Michael, I thought about how often teachers give up part of their lunch period or prep time, come in early and stay late, so they can listen to a student. No doubt I do this on a fairly regu-lar basis. But how often do I listen without judgment? Without crafting a response while they are speaking? Michael reminded me that I needed to listen on a new level. In the future, when these moments arise, I hope I can disappear.

Why It's Important

Listening is a powerful act, but we need to follow through by demonstrating that we've heard and understood the unique messages delivered by each student. This is not to say we should be offering advice or immediate solutions to every predicament. In fact, for some students, simply being heard in the moment will be enough. But the needs of each student will be different, and although some simply want to be heard, others will need us to act. Regardless, there is much to take away from each interaction, and we can use this knowledge to improve our teaching and school community. A key question explored in Cornelius Minor's (2019) book *We Got This* asks, "Because of what I've heard, how can I make active and longstanding adjustments to my classroom community, to my actual teaching, and to how the department, grade, or school operates?" (17). Minor goes on to explain that teaching is a two-way street: "Here we recognize that teaching is not monologue. It is dialogue. And after hearing what kids have to say, I've got to do something" (17).

So let's walk away from each deep listening session by letting our students' words percolate. What have we heard that might spark a change in our teaching? What ideas came through that might enhance our school culture? What might we take to our staff meetings? The more we listen, the more likely we are to find common themes in our students' concerns. As we collect these data, let's share them with other teachers and administrators. What a beautiful lesson in authentic learning—to be able to make impactful changes to our teaching and school community as a result of listening deeply to the children we serve.

Invitation and Action Steps: *Listen Deeply*

We are deluged with teaching responsibilities. Student questions, prepping for classes, grading, email, and staff meetings, Individualized Education Plan and Gifted Individualized Education Plan paperwork, and so on. The work never ends. "I'm all caught up," said no teacher ever. When our minds are racing, when we are checking boxes left and right, it often feels like we cannot breathe. How, then, can we be the kind of teacher our students need us to be? How can we be a kind and supportive colleague? The answer: by listening.

Easy to say, hard to do, right? Yep. But when we look someone in the eye and give them our full attention, the noise melts away—not permanently but long enough to be in the moment with the person in front of us. Most of the time, what students really want is to be heard and seen. They want us to recognize their frustrations, their misunderstandings. They want us to celebrate their joys, their creations, their moments of curiosity and discovery. All we need to do is listen. There is magic in hearing—deeply hearing someone speak while you both stand in the chaos of the classroom.

When you sit down to confer with a student, when you stand in the hall with them after class, or when they hand you something they've created, let the noise slip away. Show them that you hear every word. Let your body language tell them you are taking it all in. Respond, not with advice or corrections, but with a smile, or a simple, "I hear you."

Saying "I'm Sorry."

Just as I worked on my personal vulnerability when sharing with students, I began to pay closer attention to my relational vulnerability as well—my willingness to apologize to students, to give them sincere and specific compliments, and to listen deeply. I've always valued community and connection when teaching, but now I hoped to gauge my students' perception of just how important these elements are to teaching and learning.

I teach in a small, democratic (public) middle school. Our classes are mixed sixth- to eighth-grade level, and I see many of the same students for three years. Our extended time with one another gives us a chance to develop strong bonds. If I get off to a rocky start with a particular student, we have time to heal and rebuild the relationship. Sometimes, however, we may find it difficult to make a meaningful connection. One particular student tested my ability to listen and respond calmly.

Kristen entered sixth grade and quickly established herself as a boisterous, confident, witty, and often sarcastic member of the community. She wanted her voice to be heard and frequently talked over other students and teachers. One-on-one conversations about her behavior usually resulted in eye rolling and dismissive *are you finished yet?* body language. I found myself becoming more and more frustrated by her behavior, and I started to snap at her.

One day she was whispering (loudly) to another student during a class discussion, and in an angry tone I said, "Kristen, you're making it impossible for us to hear one another. Please find a different seat." She tried to explain herself, but I ignored her and went on with the lesson. Later, the student she was whispering to stopped me to explain that Kristen had been answering a question about the assignment. This student wanted me to know that Kristen was engaged in the topic; she just whispered to help clarify something. I already felt badly for the way I'd handled the situation, and now I felt worse.

I knew I needed to apologize. I thought about how I wanted things to go and realized that, in the past, I would have said something like, "Kristen, I'm sorry I snapped at you and asked you to change your seat. But you've been talking to others during lessons several times and I don't know what else to do but move you." This is not a true apology. I needed to explain that I was sorry without using the word *but*. My apology needed to be about my behavior only. This was a new challenge for me, and when I found myself sitting across from Kristen in the hallway, I was searching for the right words and being careful not to let the wrong ones slip out.

Giving a sincere apology can be hard, especially when teachers are often led to believe that having the upper hand or maintaining power and control is important. Offering an apology is an admission of fault. This jeopardizes the hierarchies that exist in most schools. Yet, breaking down these hierarchies can help improve the school environment. When student voice is valued equally to teacher voice, we are likely to have more equitable relationships in school.

Kristen sat across from me at one of the high café tables in the hall. No one else was around, but she kept her eyes moving, avoiding mine while shifting in her seat. All I needed to do here was admit that I was wrong and tell her I was sorry. "Kristen, I want you to know that I'm sorry for snapping at you in class today." I waited to see if her posture would change. It didn't; she continued to squirm and shift positions, not making eye contact. I went on, "I shouldn't have spoken to you in an angry tone and I should not have asked you to change your seat." She looked at me for the first time, as if waiting for the *but*. When it didn't come, she nodded and said, "Thanks." I went on, "I'm going to work on being more patient and reminding myself that there are many reasons a student might be whispering during a discussion. So I'm sorry, and I'll do better."

Kristen stopped shifting in her seat and she looked down at the table. "Is that it? Aren't you going to tell me what I need to do?" I shook my head and said, "This meeting is about my behavior. That's all." She didn't know what to say. We sat in silence for a few seconds, and then she said, "It's OK . . . and thanks."

Things did not become magically better for us after this encounter, but they did improve. And by the time Kristen was in eighth grade, we had a strong, trusting relationship. There were other apologies, from each of us to the other. I think we realized we were a lot alike, and this created some tension. Kristen is now in high school, and we still keep in touch.

Offering a sincere apology to Kristen went a long way toward building trust. I made that initial conversation about my mistake; had I mentioned her behavior during our meeting (like I'd done countless times before), it would have made my apology seem manipulative and disingenuous. I also believe that our willingness to sit quietly, in silence, made the experience more authentic. So often, we try to fill uncomfortable moments with words; however, sitting with the silence, especially after an adult has admitted fault, validates the interaction. We were not rushed, there were no more pressing things to get to, it wasn't something I wanted to simply get off my chest—no, this was important, and I needed to demonstrate it through words, body language, and action.

How It Impacts Students

How are teacher apologies received by students? Obviously, this depends on the situation and how genuine the apology feels. If a relationship is already established, it's more likely to go well and feel genuine. However, a heartfelt apology can also be the catalyst to a healthy teacher–student relationship. Now a tenth grader, Kristen reflects on the rarity of teacher apologies and the impact they have when they do occur.

> It seems as if it is rare that a teacher chooses to apologize for a mistake they made, especially when they have to apologize to their students. At [my high school] at least, teachers are always right. If a student chooses to contradict them, it tends to visibly upset the teacher (at least from what I've seen). However, I feel that when a teacher is willing to be vulnerable

and admit to their class that they made a mistake (a bigger mistake than a typo on a paper), the energy in the classroom shifts. The teacher is more trusted, and the students are able to view the teacher as a fellow human rather than a boss or a robot that hands out assignments and grades.

When I was in [my middle school], I had a teacher ridicule my friends & I for something we were doing during lunch. The teacher used an angry and forceful tone of voice; he was upset with us. Later, though, that same teacher pulled us aside and apologized for the way they spoke to my friends & I. I was surprised, I had never had that kind of interaction with a teacher. I felt that the interaction built my relationship with the teacher, as well as building my trust and my willingness to be vulnerable in my work & in the classroom.

Invitation and Action Steps: *Apologize*

Growing up in the '80s, I watched the TV show *Happy Days*. One of the main characters was Arthur "Fonzie" Fonzarelli—the cool guy. He was all ego. And he could not say he was sorry. When he knew he had done something wrong and was faced with the prospect of apologizing, he couldn't get the words out. Try as he might, he stuttered, "What I'm trying to say is I'm srrrr . . . I'm sorroror . . . I was wrororo . . ."

Many people cannot even get as far as Fonzie did. They will do everything in their power to avoid admitting fault, sharing some of the responsibility, and (heaven forbid) apologizing. Often, after we do some real self-reflection, we can see where we might have contributed to the frustration or hurt of a student. If that's the case, we need to find a way to offer an honest apology.

It's not easy to say, "I should have listened to you explain why the assignment was late. I reacted too quickly, and I'm sorry. Next time I will be more patient." I've found that when I apologize for my role in an event, the other party will often share what they might have done differently as well. There is a deep appreciation and respect that comes from a genuine apology.

After self-reflecting, consider offering an apology. Sure, the student or parent may have done things that were irresponsible or hurtful, but that doesn't absolve us from our role in the experience. We only have control over our own response to a situation; identifying areas where we can improve and sharing those with students and parents takes courage. And without a doubt, it builds trust.

Offering Genuine Feedback: Staff Sessions

Our principal, Dr. Jon Downs, was never a teacher. Prior to becoming an administrator, Jon was a guidance counselor. It's no surprise that his greatest strength is listening well. His abilities to hear each staff member, listen to parents, and invite students to have a voice all help in creating a strong school community. He realizes that his informal and formal observations, and subsequent feedback, have limited influence on our practice as teachers. Instead, on occasion, he encourages us to offer anonymous reflections for one another.

Near the end of the school year, we are invited to write what we appreciate about each staff member. Next, we offer suggestions on how each of us might be nudged to be a better colleague and teacher. The narratives are compiled by an administrative assistant, printed, and returned to us in a sealed envelope. We are given a week to process the feedback, and then we come together to share. It's always an emotional process but one that I feel helps strengthen our relationships with one another. It goes like this . . . we take turns orally summarizing the messages received and then we state something we would like to work on moving forward. After each staff member finishes, the rest offer specific compliments for the teacher who just spoke. It's an overwhelmingly positive experience. It's important to note that we are a small school and our staff can sit together in a single classroom. This allows us to know one another well, co-teach, and maintain open lines of communication. Those who teach in larger schools may consider offering feedback by grade level or team.

The first time I went through this process, I was emotionally exhausted. Sharing what I needed to work on wasn't terribly hard for me; strangely, it was listening to all of the compliments that made me squirm a bit. I found myself having trouble making eye contact with my colleagues as they spoke. At the time, I didn't know why I was looking away, but now it's clear. Being fully engaged in a compliment, especially (for me) when receiving one, requires a whole lot of relational vulnerability. Although I can accept your gentle critique that was written on paper, I have trouble looking you in the eye while you praise me. But I do realize that to fully accept a compliment, I need to look the giver in the eye, and say thank you. I know my colleagues appreciate me, but hearing them give specific reasons why was tough.

I've worked in divisive teaching environments, the kind where disagreements are kept quiet, where resentment builds. Carrying this kind of tension makes it difficult to come to work each day. No one wants to enter a space where feelings of anger or frustration are routine. By offering a time to share openly and honestly, Jon helped to create a more authentic school. And this is not the only real conversation we have; this process simply sets the tone for what's expected, welcomed, and embraced at our school. It says: We all see the good in one another, yet we are all fallible, and we will hold one another accountable in a supportive way. When the administration and staff are committed to purposeful, relationship-building practices among one another, it will have trickle-down effects in the classroom as well.

Offering Genuine Feedback: Conferring About Writing

I've been guilty of reading my students' work with a critical eye. It's easy to point out grammatical errors, mark sentence fragments, and suggest different word choices. But when teachers work from a deficit mindset, it will likely make students feel as though they are not capable writers. There is tremendous power in first pointing out what works. After they believe that they *can* write, they will be far more receptive to hearing how they can make it even better. In her book *Hidden Gems*, Katherine Bomer (2010) states, "My hope is that as teachers we can respond to all students' writing with astonished, appreciative, awe-struck eyes" (7). If we bring Bomer's sense of wonder to every conferring session, we are far more likely to discover the clever, witty, unique, and artistic ways our students convey their thinking.

We may also feel a discomfort when pointing out the beautiful writing our students produce. Offering feedback as we read their work, we might be tempted to simplify our response by saying, "You're a really good writer because you use lots of descriptive words." Our eyes are on their paper, and the comment doesn't sound as though it's meant for them—there's nothing special about it. However, if we pause, look them in the eye, and say, "OK, this sentence right here (read it aloud to them) captures what it means to be fourteen and longing for summer. When I read it, I am immediately whisked back to my windowless eighth-grade classroom. Your writing makes me feel alive." Giving this compliment is not easy for everyone. Looking a student in the eye and sharing this heartfelt observation may require some vulnerability on the part of the giver; it may also make the student look away in embarrassment. But no doubt, they will appreciate the specificity and recognition. They will carry that with them as they move on to the next project, knowing they have something to offer.

Imagine if we found a way to give every student that gift. No matter how much they struggle to write clearly, there are always little pieces of magic in their writing. We should be on the lookout for these, name them, celebrate them—what a wonderful way to convince emerging writers that their work can move readers.

Invitation and Action Steps: *Highlight Their Strengths*

The next time you read a student's writing, ask yourself, *If this were my project, what would I need to hear to find pride in my work? What would encourage me to keep going?* Whether I'm conferring with writers, reading their work side by side, or offering written feedback, I like to pull golden lines from their projects. I read it back to them or copy and paste it into my comments and explain why this sentence/paragraph/phrase made me think, wonder, or feel. Every writer produces golden lines, but we need to train ourselves to pay attention and seek them out.

Accepting Blame Leads to Healing

Our classroom lives can be so busy, so intense, it's nearly impossible to be aware of everything we've said in a day, not to mention our tone of voice, body language, and facial expressions. In reality, all of these things impact how our students see us and themselves. What we may intend as a casual or humorous comment could unintentionally wound. Here, teacher Jen Rand recounts an experience where, for months, she had no idea why a relationship with one of her students was strained.

In my current role as a gifted support teacher, I work with students in a much different way than I did as an English teacher and I sometimes miss direct instruction. To make up for this, I've taken on the responsibility of advising several clubs, one of which is the speech and debate team for our school. In such a competitive school district, particularly among students who are highly motivated, driven, and focused on their résumés for college applications, club leadership positions are particularly coveted.

Several years ago, a young debater applied for the role of club president and, though one of several qualified applicants, I ultimately did not select her. I wasn't aware of how upset she was about this until her parents reached out to a principal of the school asking for the decision to be revisited because, they felt, I was biased against their daughter. I did not believe their perception to be accurate; however, I had the administrator review all the club officer applications, as well as my process, and she came to the same conclusion I had. The principal's opinion did not satiate the parents and they asked to meet with me.

Over the course of the meeting, the parents revealed to me that their daughter—an excellent debater, a kind young woman, and someone I believed I had a good relationship with—felt that I had it in for her all year. They told me about an event that had happened early in the fall (this meeting was in March) that had been so upsetting to her that she had nearly quit the team. At a tournament, when she was, in my assessment, distracting some fellow (male) debaters by sitting close to them, touching them, and laughing a lot, I joked to the student that she needed to stop flirting and instead focus on improving her own speeches. In my memory of the event, she took my admonishment fine and moved on. The reality, her parents told me, was that she called them shortly after, in tears, and asked them to come pick her up. She was humiliated and told them she couldn't understand why I would say something like that to her. They told me that the impact of my assessment was deeply unfair and especially injurious because this student is raised in a culture that is physically demonstrative with friends, and at sixteen, she wasn't even dating yet. To have a respected teacher not only misinterpret her intent but call it out as such in front of two male friends, was crushing to her.

To hear that I had so thoughtlessly and dismissively hurt a student was crushing right back. I was grateful to her parents for sharing this with me and assured them I would apologize, which I was able to do the next day. This apology was not difficult to give and the student received it well. We spoke for quite some time and she was willing and able to process her lingering distress with me. I want to say the experience was good for us both, and I believe that it was. She seemed perceptibly lighter after we spoke, and we had a strong working relationship for the next year. I can say with confidence that there is little chance she would have elected to work with me in the ways she did her senior year—not only was she on the debate team, but as one of my gifted support students, she also relied upon me to serve the role of school counselor through her college application process—had I not given her a sincere and honest apology for my misstep.

It's never easy to learn that we've hurt a student. It's our default to become defensive and explain all the reasons why we never meant to offend; but impact is what matters most. So if we can recognize that our actions caused pain, and we find the humility to apologize for causing that pain, we can—as Jen demonstrated here—begin to heal fractured relationships.

Invitation and Action Steps: *Self-Reflect*

I'd been teaching for about five years when I received an angry note from a parent. She was frustrated because her daughter came home from school in tears about an assignment. The daughter didn't understand how to do the work, and apparently, I hadn't been clear about the expectations. My initial reaction was to state all the reasons why this wasn't my fault. So that's what I did. In my response, I stated how I'd given clear directions, how I offered to answer any questions (there were none), how I handed out a sheet with step-by-step directions, and how that child had left these directions at school. Clearly, I had done nothing wrong . . . or so I thought.

I ended up with a cold relationship—I was not able to establish a positive connection with this student or parent; the year must have been a frustrating one for both of them. Had I self-reflected and offered a more compassionate response, had my goal not be to defend myself, I might have salvaged the relationship. Looking back, I wish my thought process had been something like this: "OK, maybe she didn't ask for clarification because she wasn't comfortable doing so in front of the class when no one else had questions. And the fact that no one had any questions should be a red flag. Of course there were questions, but no one was comfortable enough to ask. What might this say about the culture of the classroom I'd created?" If I had offered to speak to the student over the phone to clarify the assignment, if I had spoken privately with her the next day and given her another copy of the directions, if I had offered an extension, things would likely have played out differently.

I needed to get my ego out of the equation and do what was best for the student. I allowed my insecurities and my desire to be right get in the way of maintaining a healthy learning environment for that student.

The next time you receive an email from a frustrated parent or student, ask yourself what you could have done differently. This goes against our gut reaction to defend and deflect. But we need to remember that the goal is always to establish and maintain a healthy working relationship with parents and students. By self-reflecting, we are more likely to respond in a kind, compassionate manner.

Relational vulnerability requires courage. At the surface level, things like apologies, compliments, and listening may seem easy. Some of us do these things regularly. But I wonder, are we consistently able to practice these acts in a genuine way? When we understand the importance of listening with clarity, apologizing with grace, and complimenting with specificity and sincerity, I believe we can access a new level of connection that will strengthen our school communities and set the stage for engaged learning.

LOOKING BACK   LOOKING AHEAD

Consider answering these questions in a personal journal and then discussing with a colleague:

- Reflect on a time when you apologized in school. Was your apology followed by a *but*?

- How might you plan ahead for your next apology? What can you do to make it more sincere?

- What does your practice of giving compliments look like? Do compliments happen quickly, in passing, or do they occur during conferring sessions? Consider your body language and tone of voice.

- Are your compliments general or specific?

- How might you alter your practice of giving compliments?

- When do you carve out time to listen deeply to your students?

- How do you show students that you hear them?

- When you listen, what does your body language look like?

- How might you improve your practice of listening?

DIALOGIC
VULNERABILITY

LET'S TALK—FOR REAL

As a white male teacher who grew up (and teaches) in a town that's over 80 percent white, my privilege has allowed me to avoid conversations about race and equity. I haven't needed to engage because I benefit from being part of the dominant group. Only recently have I begun to recognize my privilege and how it's contributed to my lack of action. Frankly, I'm embarrassed it took me this long to understand that by doing nothing to make change, I'm perpetuating the status quo. The guilt, frustration, and admission of my own ignorance moved me to initiate courageous conversations with my colleagues and students.

Over the years, I've danced around topics of race and equity in the classroom, touched on them briefly, and wrapped them up quickly—not because I found them unimportant, but because I found them so monumental that I didn't even know how to begin. Entering these conversations made me feel vulnerable as a teacher. Did I want to talk about race, equity, privilege, LGBTQIA+ issues with my students? Absolutely. But I was hesitant to jump in. After beginning the identity work through our Building Anti-Racist White Educators staff discussions, reading relevant books authored by people of color, and digging in for some intense self-reflection, I felt better prepared to bring these conversations into the classroom.

This is not a chapter about how and when to have tough conversations. Many others have written beautifully about this (see list in following Invitation and Action Steps on page 83). This chapter is about recognizing and embracing our own vulnerability when preparing for tough conversations.

When I started teaching in the late '90s, there were scripted lessons for tough topics at certain grade levels. When teaching our human body unit to fifth graders, we were carefully trained on what to say and what not to say. I remember being on edge and focused more on protecting the class from hearing anything they weren't supposed to hear than delving into their questions.

Rather than avoiding topics because they might make us uncomfortable, let's invite them into the safe spaces we've created for our students. Here, we begin to see the issue from a variety of perspectives. If the classroom is a space that values all the voices in the room, we may begin to see the issue through multiple lenses, and in turn, that issue may not seem so taboo. Sara Ahmed warns us of the consequences we face when avoiding tough conversations:

> It is imperative in a democracy that many voices are included in discourse, and conversations around relevant topics are not easy when it comes to negotiating everyone's individual experiences. Avoiding these conversations now—at a point in our students' lives when they are the most able to consider new perspectives—will yield a generational ignorance we can't afford for the future. Ignorance is not bliss. Ignorance is a luxury of the privileged and a barrier to the unnoticed and undeserved. (Ahmed 2018, xv)

Just as each of us should know our boundaries when sharing personal experiences, we also need to gauge the readiness of each class to discuss certain topics. Any time I'm unsure whether or not to broach a topic or event, I consult my colleagues. Bouncing my ideas off of those I trust helps me sort out the *why* behind my conundrum. After chatting with colleagues, I typically feel better about my decision. Most of the time, I'm supported and encouraged to move forward with the discussion. But there have been times when I've decided to pull back the reins and do some learning of my own before bringing the topic to class.

Prior to engaging in meaningful discussions with students, it's important to do some identity work ourselves. It wasn't until I began to recognize my own privilege that I could even begin to effectively facilitate conversations around issues of social justice.

My student survey on dialogic vulnerability included a general question about tough conversations and two Likert scale questions assessing their comfort level with tackling race and LGBTQIA+ issues. I knew we'd be engaging in tough conversations throughout the school year, so I wanted to gauge how their thinking might change. By asking the first question, I was hoping to discover how tense conversations impacted engagement and classroom community. Here's the question:

HAVE ANY OF YOUR TEACHERS FACILITATED DISCUSSIONS WHERE OPINIONS DIFFER AND EMOTIONS RUN STRONG? IF SO, HOW DOES THIS IMPACT YOUR ENGAGEMENT IN THE CLASS? ALSO, HOW DOES IT IMPACT THE OVERALL SENSE OF COMMUNITY?

Most students replied that they had experienced these types of conversations at some point in their schooling. The overwhelming majority believed that these types of discussions increased engagement. They found it difficult to tune out intense conversations. Additionally, they felt that although folks might be divided in their thinking during the discussion, these conversations ultimately strengthened the classroom and school community. Here's a sampling of their responses:

> Yes, and it got everyone more engaged because there wasn't a blockade between our internal emotions and the discussion. It made everyone feel more like a family, in my opinion.

> Yes, and I think that it makes me much more engaged, because I feel like I have to defend what I think about the topic, and I think that it brings everyone involved closer together.

> It definitely strengthens the community and I feel more engaged. It's hard to zone out during an intriguing conversation.

After examining student responses to my surveys, it was clear that engaging in dialogic vulnerability led to the following trends:

- ○ increases student engagement
- ○ encourages student voice
- ○ strengthens community.

Another encouraging data point came from the Likert scales. These demonstrated an increased comfort level (from only September to January) when discussing LGBTQIA+ topics and issues of race. In just six months, students who were reluctant to engage in these conversations began to demonstrate a willingness to listen and learn. Though they still may not have spoken up in class, the idea of listening, exploring, and being OK with the discomfort is a huge step in the right direction. It's clear that when teachers responsibly engage in crucial conversations, we are giving students the opportunity to interact—in a meaningful way—with real-world issues.

Preparing Ourselves for Tough Conversations

When we have something important to explore with our students, it can be difficult to wait. But if it's really that critical, we want to be sure we are prepared to lead our students through the process. It's unreasonable to assume that we can guide students through these conversations without having experienced them ourselves. Initially, I thought reading and reflecting on books about race and equity was ample preparation; I was wrong. I needed to explore the ideas presented with others. I needed to grapple with my own privilege, my own biases. Fortunately, I had colleagues who were willing to learn alongside me.

Building Antiracist White Educators:
A Staff Model for Dialogic Vulnerability

BARWE provides tools for teachers to address their own biases and work together to examine classroom and schoolwide practices and how they impact students of color. From their website: "White teachers, even those with experience and compassion, can unconsciously cause pain to students of color in their classrooms. We believe that through consistent study and reflection, we can slowly address our own unconscious biases and make changes so we can better support the academic, social and emotional well-being of our students of color" (BARWE 2021).

The organization provides a framework for discussion, releasing new questions and topics each month: "This Reading and Inquiry Series provides a monthly set of tools for learning, introspection and having conversations about issues of racism in our schools, classrooms and communities. We hope that through regular reflection and conversation, you can get better at recognizing and resisting your biases and the impact they have on your students and colleagues of color" (BARWE 2021).

Our small school holds a BARWE meeting each month, and anywhere from four to eight teachers attend. Small groups are ideal, as it gives everyone a chance to be heard. We've discussed everything from what it means to develop an anti-racist identity as a white educator to how we can identify and challenge implicit bias in our own practice. These conversations are difficult and require us to embrace discomfort. In our meetings, we are consistently examining our practices, admitting fault, and recognizing the pain we may have caused our students of color. But we are also reminding one another that when we make decisions about curriculum, discipline, and other school policies, we need to consider it all through our BARWE lens.

Practicing these conversations with colleagues helps prepare us for the dialogic vulnerability we will embrace in the classroom. But there is another benefit to participating in BARWE. Engaging in crucial conversations with colleagues helps deepen our connections. Too often, schools attempt to build community through icebreakers and social gatherings. Although these activities can help us get to know one another on a surface level, working through tough conversations, sharing our biases, admitting fault, and searching for ways to better ourselves and our school lead to true community. We see one another more fully, as flawed, frustrated, and inspired people who are coming together to support one another and our students. That's the bedrock of a growth and connection.

Engaging in dialogic vulnerability with other teachers is a critical step in the process of preparing for tough conversations with our students:

> If we want to teach students to become compassionate, complex thinkers, we must first muddle through this work ourselves. Otherwise, we may not be prepared for the outcomes: the fight or flight, the tears, the crawling of skin, the desire to shake the tables . . . the more we are able to be introspective upfront, the more comfortable we may become with the discomfort of powerful discussions that can move us all to new levels as learners and critical thinkers, and to sometimes Herculean feats of humanity. (Ahmed 2018, xxvi)

Being with teachers who talked openly about race and who were willing to examine their own biases taught me that I was not alone in wanting to bring these conversations into the classroom.

Invitation and Action Steps: *Establish a BARWE or Social Justice Group with Colleagues*

The BARWE group has impacted my teaching and collegial relationships. It has provided a framework for seeing my school and curriculum through a new lens. The wonderful thing about BARWE is that the structure for each meeting is laid out for teachers. On their site, you can find monthly articles, videos, and a framework that teachers can use for each meeting. Organizing a reading group where students, parents, and teachers meet monthly to discuss a social justice–themed book is another option. Here are some resources to get you started:

- Use the resources found at https://www.barwe215.org/ to help establish a BARWE group.

○ Consider organizing a social justice book group. Learning for Justice provides articles and guidance on how to initiate this in your school. Check out https://www.learningforjustice.org.

○ Yet another resource is Courageous Conversation, which offers protocol for engaging in dialogue about race. They offer seminars, training for school leaders, and can help design curriculum. More can be found here: https://courageousconversation.com/about/.

Student Voice + Tough Conversations = Engagement

I needed to be thoughtful about how to invite and facilitate discussions around race and equity with middle schoolers. How could I, as a white teacher who grew up in a mostly white town, effectively lead conversations about race and equity? I decided to begin with an explanation and then follow with a framework for future conversations.

I told my students that I recognized how often they brought up topics about race and equity but that I'd failed to give these topics the time and attention they deserve. That would now change. I introduced Glenn E. Singleton's and Curtis Linton's Four Agreements from the Courageous Conversations About Race protocol: stay engaged, experience discomfort, speak your truth, and expect and accept nonclosure. It's important to note that although we would likely discuss non-race-related issues as well, the four agreements would only be used to discuss topics about race.

Next, I asked students to complete a quick write that would be collected and used to generate discussion topics. Why ask students and not simply choose a list of topics on my own? Because just as listening is a necessary component when building relationships, it is just as critical when deciding what is worth discussing. As Sara K. Ahmed reminds us, "Skilled listeners have a stance that shows the speaker they care. You cannot fake this stance. You have to genuinely care and commit. That's why I implore teachers to ask kids what's in *their* news, not to impose only our news on them" (2018, 129).

We routinely impose a great deal on our students. Their days are filled with teacher-directed rules, objectives, and lessons. Any time we have the chance to invite student voice, we should.

> When we allow kids to be curious about topics they care
> and wonder about, and when we are honest with them, they
> give their whole selves to the listening. And if we enter into
> a brave conversation with someone, we must commit to the
> path it may take and be authentic in our listening so we send
> the message that the other person's ideas, thoughts, and
> feelings are legitimized. My bet is your commitment will be
> reciprocated. (129)

I kept my prompt open-ended but provided things to think about as they wrote:

WHAT COURAGEOUS CONVERSATIONS WOULD YOU LIKE TO EXPLORE IN THIS CLASSROOM?

○ What topics do we typically avoid in school that should be addressed?

○ What topics do you feel more students and teachers should be aware of?

○ Whose voices are being silenced? Left out? Ignored?

As is often the case, my students surprised me with their frankness, knowledge, honesty, and wisdom. Here is a sampling of their responses:

○ how to confront friends/family/adults when they make hurtful comments

○ how are groups that are marginalized represented in the books we read?

○ the importance of the words we choose to use

○ ways to support the LGBTQIA+ community

○ gender stereotypes

- ○ climate change
- ○ immigration policies
- ○ mental health: where and how to seek help
- ○ equal pay in the workplace.

Some students went beyond a list and shared a bit more about their thinking:

> I think having these conversations is more than a good idea. I would rather learn about issues that may be scary now rather than when I'm 20.

> I do know a lot about gender, race, and LGBTQIA+ issues in the United States, but I want to know how these issues look in other countries.

> We are talking about climate change, but not enough for people to actually start doing something about it.

While reading through their quick writes, I was reminded of the power of writing as a means to hear all voices in the classroom. Had I asked students to respond orally to my prompt, I likely would have heard from no more than five different students. The rest would have remained silent, too uncomfortable to share their thoughts with the group. Allowing students to write their questions, thoughts, and ideas enabled me to see what everyone was thinking. It also gave me a clearer focus of what to look for when searching for mentor texts. Rather than pulling an article I was interested in, I could use their interests to guide my search.

Later that evening, I read an online *New York Times* article about a Penn State football player (Penn State University is located just blocks from our school, and football is paramount here) who'd just received a racist letter from a fan. Jonathan Sutherland is a sophomore on the football team. He happens to wear his hair in dreadlocks, and apparently this upset the fan. The letter commended Sutherland for his excellent play but quickly turned offensive and racist: "Though the athletes of today are superior to those in my days; we miss the clean-cut young men and women from those days. Watching the Idaho game, we couldn't help but notice your—well—awful hair." The letter was all over social media, and Sutherland's teammates called out the racist messages. I decided to share the letter in class—it was local and relevant and could serve as a mentor text for our sports journalism class.

Many students gasped as I read the letter aloud; some asked if it was real or a joke. Several students asked why his hair mattered so much to this man. One student, though angry with the letter, tried to explain why the man wrote it:

> So this guy is sitting in his home, remembering a time when everyone looked pretty much the same on the field. Same haircuts, same pre-game suits. And now he sees guys with long hair, and it bothers him. It bothers him because he doesn't like people who are different. And he actually thinks writing this letter is a good thing. This guy thinks he's doing Sutherland a favor. It's crazy.

Another student wondered why Sutherland was targeted when other players wear long hair:

> There are plenty of players with long hair. I wonder why he chose to write to a Black player. There have been white Penn State players with long hair. Why didn't they get a letter?

And that comment led to further discussion about biases. How often do we make comments that are not intended to hurt, but do? Comments that reflect our biases? This letter was blatantly racist, and my students recognized that, but how often do we speak or write things that are racist without our knowing it? After everyone had a chance to express their anger and frustration with the letter, I asked, "So how do we respond to this? Should we? Does it matter?" Some students said the man was set in his ways, and it wouldn't make a difference. Others observed that, yes, it matters, and any time a racist comment is made, a strong response is needed; otherwise, things won't ever change.

Wrapping up our conversation without a planned action or response was frustrating for all of us. We agreed that nothing would be solved that day but bringing the conversation to light was a first step. Yet, it still felt awkward to end the conversation and simply return to our independent writing projects.

Later that evening, I reflected on the experience. I pictured my students reluctantly transitioning to their projects—their body language had told me they had more to say. I regretted not offering them another opportunity to write and reflect on our discussion. Did I cut the conversation short because I was uncomfortable? Because I didn't know where to go next? Because I was afraid of saying the wrong thing? Maybe it was my white privilege revealing itself yet again: Because of my position as a white male in a mostly white school, did I not feel the urgency necessary to press on?

I decided to revisit the conversation during another class period. I apologized for cutting the initial discussion short. I explained how, since our last conversation, I'd been thinking about how I've responded—or failed to respond—to racist remarks in my own life. I shared memories of relatives who'd made racist comments and how I was embarrassed to admit that I hadn't always spoken up. I saw heads nod and a few hands shoot up. Several students mentioned hearing racist comments at family gatherings but not knowing how to respond. A few students said that these comments are not tolerated in their homes and that they would have no problem calling people out and explaining how damaging these comments can be. But most admitted remaining silent, however angry they might have been. We did agree that, even if it's difficult, we must speak up. I suggested that the next time any of us hears a racially insensitive remark, we need to (at minimum) say, "Hearing that comment makes me uncomfortable." Though that alone is not enough, it is the first step in taking a stand, because remaining silent allows the oppression to persist.

When Teachers Are Unconditionally Themselves

Though there are specific moments of dialogic vulnerability that may stand out in our memories, there may also be teachers whose classrooms are ongoing forums for vulnerable conversation. In these rooms, dialogic vulnerability is a way of being; it is not a specific unit or lesson but rather a commitment to daily, vulnerable teaching. High school student Emma reflects on a teacher who embraced dialogic vulnerability as part of everyday teaching.

During my sophomore year of high school, I enrolled in a class called Problems That Persist which was a social studies credit all about how our perspectives intertwine into every little thing we do. From the start, it was pretty clear that I would have to put myself out there and that made me nervous. I have a big personality and I am usually an open book, however everyone has some part of themselves that they grapple with and the thought that I would be leaving it all out there for people to misconstrue and judge was daunting. So on the first day of class when I walked into the classroom dreading the tables and potential list of assigned seats, instead, a circle of single chairs wrapped around the middle of the room with the teacher ready to share every part of her life with us, you would guess my surprise!

I had never had a teacher so comfortably share life experiences, struggles, worries for the year (as it was their first-year teaching at my school), mission, and overarching goals, I was impressed. Looking back, I realize just how hard this must have been, and how no matter how many smiles and laughs they shared with us, they probably weren't comfortable at all.

That example that they set from the get-go was incredible, something I had never really seen in a teacher before and really drilled it into our head that it's okay to share and to want to be vulnerable with this group because we will be close and we will share that vulnerability, treasure it, and most importantly, keep it confidential. It was a first to me that I had never witnessed prior to that classroom experience and that community precedent we set has never looked back.

For a student, being able to see a teacher set that example for the first time was so refreshing. I have been so lucky

in that I have been able to have many amazing relationships with different teachers over the years but this teacher
stood out above all because of the trust and personal connection that she instilled in each of us on that first day.
There is something so encouraging about how this teacher
took their vulnerability and made it a strength instead.
Every day in this class, before we went into the appropriate subject matter for the day, we would start the first few
minutes with a vulnerability activity. This teacher felt so
strongly about making sure the classroom felt like a second
home that she told us from the start that striving for vulnerability is almost as important as anything. I saw this teacher
pour her heart into these activities, and slowly I saw how
my peers began to react to that. I recognized that this was
a safe place for me to share my story, to be comfortable in
my own skin.

Thriving off of vulnerability can take a long time. Now, I
see that I am still working to accept vulnerability for all that
it is, but having a teacher model that outlook on life was cap-
tivating. To this day, that class was one of the best classes I
have ever taken. Through this class and the opportunities I
had to tell my stories, hear others' stories, and listen to my
peer's stories, I found a passion for deliberation and for all
things communication.

There was never an exact moment in time where I saw this
teacher be vulnerable, and that was what made this experience just that more special. I felt that every time I walked
into that classroom and sat down, vulnerability just flowed
through the discussion. That, above anything else will be
something I take with me always, that willingness I saw from
that teacher to be unconditionally themselves.

It's clear that Emma's experience with this teacher affected her on many
levels. Not only did she grow in her ability to express herself, she was able to
connect with her classmates and discover her passion for communication. Emma

is now in college, majoring in journalism. Her teacher's commitment to dialogic vulnerability demonstrates the connection among all three dimensions. She began the class with personal vulnerability, which led to relational vulnerability, which made it much easier for the class to be dialogically vulnerable with one another. When this occurs, the learning reaches all parts of us: a better understanding of self, authentic connections with others, and deep engagement with content.

Invitation and Action Steps:
Make Student Voice a Priority

After laying the groundwork for tough conversations, we need to think about what topics we need to discuss. Freewriting is a great way to mine the questions, wonderings, and frustrations that are percolating in our students. When we write freely without the pressure of points, grades, or presentations, when we know the writing is our own and that we only need to share if we choose to, we are likely to discover ideas that energize. Because every school and classroom culture is different, each teacher must decide what topics their particular class is ready to discuss. Recalling Brené Brown's message about boundaries, we must define what's OK and what's not OK; school leadership comes into play here as well. It's important to know how well you'll be supported by your administration when facilitating difficult conversations.

Explain that you want this classroom to be a place where we can ask difficult questions, work through real-world problems, and discuss tough topics. Emphasize that, through writing, we will be able to share our thoughts, ideas, questions, and opinions. Tell students that some of our topics will come directly from the books and articles we read, but many will come from us. Start with a freewrite, and use the following prompts to get them started:

- What topics do we typically avoid that should be addressed?
- What topics do you feel more students and teachers should be aware of?
- Whose voices are being silenced? Left out? Ignored?

Gather their responses and look them over. Are there topics that were noted by several students? Which topics are you comfortable addressing? Are there ideas that—before bringing them forward in class—need to be run by a colleague? An administrator? Additionally, consider reading some of the many wonderful resources about how to have difficult conversations in the classroom:

- ○ *Not Light, but Fire: How to Lead Meaningful Race Conversations in the Classroom* by Matthew R. Kay (2018)
- ○ *Being the Change: Lessons and Strategies to Teach Social Comprehension* by Sara K. Ahmed (2018)
- ○ *The Civically Engaged Classroom: Reading, Writing, and Speaking for Change* by Mary Ehrenworth, Pablo Wolfe, and Marc Todd (2021)
- ○ *Social Justice Talk: Strategies for Teaching Critical Awareness* by Chris Hass (2020)

Leaning In Together

When a traumatic event occurs, be it a local or national event, there is no way to keep it out of school. Though we can carry on as usual in the classroom, avoiding any discussion of the topic, the event will be whispered about in the hallways, shared on busses, and debated during lunch. So we have the choice to separate ourselves from the occurrence, allowing the students to share among themselves, or we can allow for thoughtful conversation to help process the event. In some schools, teachers may be afraid of saying the wrong thing, and they may even be explicitly told by administrators to avoid the topic altogether.

I believe it's unnatural for caring communities to ignore tragic events. Students and teachers benefit from processing the news together in an age-appropriate and civil manner. But this requires dialogic vulnerability on the part of the teacher. We will likely be dealing with a visceral reaction to the event and talking about it may be emotional. Still, inviting these conversations into our school demonstrates to our students that we are an authentic school, one that wraps our collective arms around one another and experiences the range of human emotions.

Here, middle school social studies teacher Dot takes us through her reaction and creative response to the 2018 Parkland shooting.

In my practice as an educator, I am fortunate to work in a school that encourages teachers to practice freely as professionals. We are given extensive creative license in our subject areas. Although I teach multiple subjects, social studies tends to be the subject where I feel most vulnerable with my students. History is a subjective curation of events told from distinct perspectives and the ones that are chosen for the classroom are immensely important. Although social studies teachers are told to be apolitical and neutral, our curricula either reinforce or break cultural norms and understandings that themselves are political. Nothing about social studies is neutral. It has taken me a majority of seven years as a teacher to become more comfortable with that. Even then, I am still taken off guard by certain subjects.

Shortly after the Parkland school shooting in 2018, I felt an obligation to address the topic of gun control and gun violence in the United States. I did not want to give a lesson on the different perspectives, as that seemed too passive. So in a class analyzing the social issues around the Harry Potter series, I decided to have the students debate the merits of gun control and wand usage. Preparing for this assignment, I was terrified of parent backlash and created multiple announcements and sign-offs to go home. I was also terrified of what the students would be researching on their school-issued computers, especially after a significant mass casualty event at a school. I was even more anxious about the fact that I had made the decision to invite other teachers to the students' scheduled debates.

My students dove into action and dutifully prepared their arguments and rebuttals with a fearless dedication that I had not expected. During the debate, they presented their side's argument civilly and articulately with large amounts of research cited throughout their discussions. My fear, while justified, seemed to shortchange the dedication that my students

> had to learning about the topic. This debate became a stan-
> dard feature of my Harry Potter studies course, as students
> who had heard about the debate requested to participate in
> it. Through each iteration of the debate, I feel as though I
> strengthen my relationship with the students. I talk with them
> through their sticking points, I answer their questions when
> they seem in disbelief of a topic or statistic, and I hear out
> their anxieties about speaking in front of each other. There
> was a greater mutual trust between most of the students and
> myself after this assignment. My fear toward the assignment,
> which I voiced to the students, and the students' passion for
> learning about the topic allowed us so many opportunities to
> learn about each other and have candid conversations.

Dot's transparency with students and parents helped them understand her intentions while also humanizing her as a teacher. It's not common—at least in my experience—for teachers to admit that they are afraid, sad, or worried. Of course, we are free to feel this way outside of school, and teachers often let loose with their real feelings during lunch break and Friday happy hours, but what about in the classroom? Yes, we need to be strong for our students, and yes, we need to lead in a way that makes them feel safe, but we also need to model what it's like to be a real human being dealing with real-world issues. Finding that balance is difficult, but sinking into meaningful conversations during trying times will undoubtedly be a powerful learning experience for everyone involved. I also believe that it has the potential to strengthen individual and community relationships. These conversations will not be forgotten.

Anja: *Getting Comfortable with Discomfort*

As an eighth grader, Anja signed up for a course called Bridging Divides. The course—co-taught by a middle school English teacher and a high school social studies teacher—took middle and high school students through deliberative conversations around race and social justice issues. The course was an exercise in dialogic vulnerability for all parties. Here's the course description:

Sound public decisionmaking requires members of a diverse society to come together to share differing perspectives, to listen for understanding, to examine the historical, social, cultural, legal, and political roots of complex issues, and to address challenges collectively in order to effect sustainable change. Yet, we rarely have opportunities to examine our own beliefs or engage in authentic, respectful conversations about difficult issues with those outside of our own circles. This course is designed to offer students opportunities to connect with people whose perspectives and lived experiences, past and present, may differ greatly from their own and to consider issues of diversity and social justice that impact our communities. Students will explore issues of division, discrimination, and inequality through a variety of learning activities, primary texts, guest speakers, and deliberative conversations that may challenge their own understanding, assumptions, and biases. The keystone experience of the course will be a weeklong journey to Birmingham, Selma, and Montgomery, Alabama, during which students will visit historic locations from the Civil Rights Movement, meet activists who work for social justice in their communities and beyond, connect with Birmingham middle and high school students through deliberative conversations on relevant issues, and develop questions to guide their continued learning and work. Following this immersive experience, students will have the opportunity to turn their learning and questions into civic action by designing or contributing to a project that helps to bridge a divide and/or remedy a social justice issue in their school, community or nation.

Anja, like most students who took the course, was deeply impacted by the experience. Here, she reflects on what it was like to get comfortable with being uncomfortable:

I believe our Bridging Divides class relied heavily on the idea of vulnerability. We had many conversations centered around very personal things including race, sexual orientation, and gender. These conversations encouraged us to be vulnerable, and as a group we established rules to make the space feel like a safe place. We were also encouraged to be vulnerable in our written reflections knowing only our teachers (whom I trust very much) would be reading them. The fact that my teachers were also willing to be vulnerable gave the class a different dynamic. A saying that my teachers repeated quite a lot in the class was "lean into discomfort." Being vulnerable is often extremely uncomfortable and this saying reminded us to feel that discomfort, and grow rather than shying away from it.

Because Bridging Divides really embraced the idea of dialogic vulnerability, we were able to have focused and productive conversations. These conversations had real emotions rather than just facts. Also I found myself "leaning into discomfort" more often in different settings. For example, I brought up some of the hard conversations we were having in class to my parents and outside friends. The idea of leaning into discomfort was really the reason I was able to do my final project on Mass Incarceration. For this project my partner and I had to present in front of about 400 people. Presenting was a nerve wracking and uncomfortable experience that also put me in a place of vulnerability. However, I think that my school and I personally gained a lot from that experience. I believe that if in Bridging Divides there hadn't been that emphasis on getting comfortable being uncomfortable and allowing yourself to be vulnerable, I wouldn't have been able to give that presentation.

This course was the embodiment of dialogic teaching. It invited all parties to bring themselves fully into the conversation. Although more traditional classes might examine the historical components of the content and require students to demonstrate their understanding, this course went a step further by asking students to examine themselves and understand how history has shaped who they are today and who they might become in the future. This kind of deeply personal learning can only take place in spaces where dialogic vulnerability is part of the classroom culture.

Invitation and Action Steps:
Lean into Discomfort with Students

When I first felt moved to bring issues of race and equity into the classroom, I gathered relevant newspaper articles, essays, and books. I was ready to go. I felt the urgency and I was driven to share my questions and concerns with students. How can we confront racism in our community? What's the most productive way to respond to hate? But I needed to pump the brakes. As mentioned previously, I needed to do some identity work and take a hard look at my own biases. It was also important for me to lay the groundwork in my classroom. Before we can have meaningful conversations with students, especially those that will require risk and vulnerability, we need to establish norms for discussion.

Learning for Justice provides so many powerful tools for preparing teachers and students to engage in tough conversations. Use the resource "Let's Talk!" to get started. This resource provides before, during, and after strategies for engaging students in critical conversations. It also offers ways to establish classroom norms that will help students feel safe. Questions like "What do we want our conversation to look like? Feel like? Sound Like?" help students understand the expectations and ways of being in the classroom. The full resource is free and can be found here: https://www.learningforjustice.org/magazine/publications/lets-talk.

Invitation and Action Step:
Get Involved with Curriculum Planning

Every district's procedure for developing curriculum is different. Some involve teachers and some do not. If you have the ability to be part of a curriculum design committee, volunteer. Share resources, and be vocal about the need to incorporate ongoing dialogue about issues of race and equity. Emphasize that lessons on Martin

Luther King Jr. Day and Black History Month are not enough. Consider how we can consistently examine our practice, our lessons, our classroom conversations through an equity lens.

Do what you can to influence your district's curriculum. Ask to be part of a planning or design committee. If your district doesn't involve teachers in the design process, ask to meet with school leaders or those in charge of curriculum. Share resources and talk about the importance of establishing and maintaining a focus on equity.

We may certainly feel vulnerable when we dive into tough conversations. But they are necessary, and through our discussions, we will likely learn that our students—in general—are less afraid than we are. We need to trust the process and continue to create time to speak and write about issues that make us uncomfortable until our discomfort motivates us to act.

In schools or classrooms where personal and relational vulnerability are part of everyday practice, dialogic vulnerability becomes a natural extension of our practice. Classrooms become places with a focus on getting real—real topics, real discussions, real dialogue, real teachers. We need more students leaving classes with Emma's takeaway: "I felt that every time I walked into that classroom and sat down, vulnerability just flowed through the discussion. That, above anything else will be something I take with me always, that willingness I saw from that teacher to be unconditionally themselves."

LOOKING BACK  LOOKING AHEAD

Consider answering these questions in a personal journal and then discussing with a colleague:

- Have you begun to examine your implicit biases? If so, how have they impacted your instruction and the way you interact with students?

- How will recognizing these biases begin to change the way you teach?

- When have you experienced dialogic vulnerability?

- What types of conversations have you avoided in the classroom?

- What conversations would you like to invite but are hesitant to introduce?

- What are some topics that would offer a safe way to ease into dialogic vulnerability?

- Are there colleagues you might lean on for support as you begin this endeavor?

- Are there ways you could co-facilitate (with another teacher) crucial conversations?

- What conversations have you had among teachers that required dialogic vulnerability?

- How might you organize a teacher group to engage in crucial conversations?

VULNERABILITY
AND
SCHOOL CULTURE

Although each dimension of vulnerability can be identified, singularly, in the classroom, the various dimensions often act as building blocks for one another. For example, sharing a personal story (personal vulnerability) may lead to a stronger relationship (relational vulnerability), which will likely allow for more authentic conversations (dialogic vulnerability). Sometimes, they can all occur in the space of a single class period. These magical moments might be rare, but when they happen, they can be transformational.

Synergistic Moments

The room was silent—the good kind of silent—where twenty middle schoolers were staring into the pages of twenty different books. On this day, most seemed locked in; I didn't notice any wandering eyes or repetitive glances at the clock. After kneeling to talk with Catherine about the dilemma her favorite character faced, I noticed Alli sitting quietly, her book closed on the table. She rested her chin on her palm and stared off toward the corner of the room. A week earlier, Alli, one who only recently considered herself an avid reader, asked me for a copy of *The Outsiders* (Hinton 2016). She told me that someone had recommended it, and she wanted to give it a shot.

"Did you finish?" I whispered.

"No," she said. "I just need a minute." And then the tears came. Her favorite character had died. "I've never felt this way about a book before. I think I'm overreacting. It feels silly."

"I'm sorry you're upset right now. No, you're not overreacting. It's so cool you found a book to connect with so deeply," I said.

She left the room, said she needed some time to compose herself. Later that morning, I saw her sitting in the hallway talking to another student. As she gestured, I imagined her relaying the events from the book to her listener. Sure enough, as I walked by, she said, "This book! I can't get it out of my head."

During the final period of the day, I received a text from a colleague just down the hall—Alli's advisor and social studies teacher. It said, "Alli just made me cry." After school, I touched base with my colleague who relayed Alli's animated retelling of the story, the loss of a character who felt like a friend, and her inability to shake the feeling that, suddenly, the act of reading was just elevated to a whole new level.

Reflecting on this transformative reading experience, I wondered about the variables that needed to fall into place to make something like this happen. First of all, she needed the freedom to select a book she was interested in reading. Had her reading selections been dictated by a teacher who felt that *The Outsiders* should only be taught in freshman English class, this sixth grader wouldn't have had the opportunity to read the book in school. Are there elements of the book she may not fully grasp? Probably. Might she benefit from rereading it again as an older student? Sure. But after witnessing the deep connection she made with the story, I wouldn't ever want to deny her—or any child—such an experience.

She also benefited from being part of a classroom community that embraced vulnerability. Not every classroom invites and embraces emotional reactions. The fact that Alli was able to shed tears about a book and was subsequently comforted by middle school students and teachers speaks volumes about the school culture. An acquaintance sat with her in the hall, listening to her break down the reasons why this character resonated with her. The social studies teacher shed a tear as he listened to her explain how, finally, she understood the power of *story*. The students and teachers allowed her to *feel* publicly and supported her while she sorted through the range of emotions.

Alli found me the next morning, held up a wad of folded papers, and said, "I've written pages about this! Pages!" There was no assignment given—she did this on her own, because she felt moved to write.

Alli said she was willing to share this experience with the class (not everyone knew why she was upset and had to leave the classroom). During our next session, Alli and I retold the story together—from the moment I noticed her staring off into the corner of the room, to when she needed to leave to regain her composure. She smiled as she tried to articulate the feeling she had when the emotions hit:

> It was weird to feel myself getting upset after reading something that never actually happened in real life. The character isn't real—I know that—but for some reason, he still felt like a friend.
>
> After I realized he died, all I could think about was my other favorite character. I needed to know if he was going to be ok. I actually skipped ahead in the book to find out.
>
> I used to tell people that *Harry Potter* was my favorite book, but it never made me feel like this. I will never forget this book.

Next, I shared two emotional experiences from my own reading life: once alone at home, when I threw a tattered classic across the room before reluctantly picking it up with shaky hands to read its final pages. And another time, in class, when I was reading aloud and couldn't go on—I dropped my head and handed the book off to a student who took over while I ran my sleeve across my face. I asked if anyone else had a similar reading experience. Hands shot up and students shared memories of books they'd read years ago but whose characters remain tattooed on their hearts. Most told their stories with smiles, as if remembering the escapades of a long-lost friend. A few spoke quietly, with a reverence reserved for personal moments.

Though the focus of this book is on the impact that teacher vulnerability has on student learning experiences, this particular act was initiated by a student, and it gave me the opportunity to share memories of my own reading life. Alli's vulnerability inspired me to be vulnerable, which inspired her classmates to open up. In the right environment, vulnerability can be contagious.

I've wondered how teacher vulnerability might impact students academically. Is there a connection between teacher vulnerability and academic growth? It's clear to me that when I am vulnerable and authentic, my relationships with students are strengthened. And strong teacher–student relationships provide a foundation for learning. But I've also noticed that—in classrooms that embrace vulnerability—many students are more willing to grapple with what it means to be *real* when we read and write. And just as *real* writing is a catalyst to quality writing, experiencing emotional resonance while reading propels us toward engaged reading.

Do all students need to cry in class to prove their love of reading? Of course not. Readers will be moved in different ways: some may smile and laugh quietly, others may feel a sadness they only share with a friend, and a few may be quietly inspired to seek out every title written by a specific author. Regardless of their reaction, schools and teachers need to create spaces where students feel safe to feel the range of emotions when reacting to the written word.

Alli allowed herself to be personally vulnerable while reading in school. As she processed her feelings around this reading experience (with students and teachers), she enriched our community. The follow-up conversation about our reading histories allowed for dialogic vulnerability. This all unfolded in an organic way, touching on all three dimensions of vulnerability.

The Power of Hearing All Voices

There is power in gathering together as a school community. There is even greater power when we let the students lead. Though I realize that our school is a small one and that not every institution can gather together in a space where all voices are heard, I believe that it is possible for schools to allow for greater student voice. It's possible for grade levels or subgroups to find common time to gather and share ideas.

Our school comes together every Thursday for a thirty-minute all-school meeting. Each session is run by two student facilitators (students, along with a designated teacher, meet weekly to plan the agenda). The student facilitators welcome the large group and share the norms of our meeting. Next, we go through the agenda together.

When families or visitors ask to spend time in our school, we always invite them to come during an all-school meeting. These meetings reveal the heart of our school; they demonstrate the value of student voice, the power of hearing everyone's opinions, and the impact of genuine compliments. But these meetings are not always smooth and peaceful; they can also get messy. Sometimes, the discussion becomes heated, and students say things they later regret. For example, I can recall a discussion about the school dress code. Several students were upset by the fact that the dress code seemed to be targeting females, and the students were pushing for a reworking of this school policy. During the conversation, their anger was palpable. They had been hurt by this policy and we could all see and feel it in their body language and tone of voice. This kind of emotional display is surprising to our visitors. Many have not witnessed this kind of interaction in a school setting—especially not in such a public forum. And there are times when teachers do jump in and redirect the conversation. But it's clear that students have far more room to voice their opinions, concerns, and suggestions than in more traditional school settings.

Regardless of what happens during the old and new business sessions, we end each meeting with kudos. This never gets old. Hearing students and staff shower one another with compliments along with stories of kindness and bravery witnessed throughout the week is uplifting. Typically, we walk away from our all-school meetings feeling inspired, cared for, and supported.

Examples of kudos shared by middle schoolers and staff:

> I'd like to give kudos to Jared for helping me out during math today. I was so confused at first, but after working with him, I got it.

> Kudos to Madison for making me laugh at recess. I was feeling pretty low when I got to school, but after spending time with her at recess, things are better.

> Kudos to Stacy for making science fun today. The way she teaches with all that energy makes me love her classes.

> Big kudos to Henry for sticking around after class today. He noticed we'd all left a mess, and he helped me clean things up.

To establish and maintain a strong school community, we need to find ways to come together, listen as a group, voice our thoughts, and recognize one another's good deeds. We need to talk about real issues together, learn to listen and respond to those with differing opinions, and react in a thoughtful way. How can we ask our students to become kind, brave, and vocal human beings if we don't offer them the space to practice? All-school meetings provide the necessary framework to make this a reality.

Invitation and Action Steps: *Implement Regular All-School (or All–Grade Level) Meetings*

Find a teacher who is willing to organize an all-school meeting committee. Students in the committee work together to establish an agenda and facilitate the meetings. Each meeting should follow a clear structure, and we've found it helps to remind everyone of the norms at the beginning of each get-together. Our meetings are always thirty minutes in length. Meetings might encompass the entire school, grade level groups, or a team.

- Quote of the week: A student reads a quote that they feel is important.
- Announcements: Upcoming events, school and community performances, and so on are announced.
- Birthdays: Student and staff birthdays for the week are listed.
- Old business: Topics that came up during a previous meeting that still need attention are addressed.
- New business: New topics for discussion (examples: dress code discussion, music during class, phone use in school) are addressed.
- Random acts of kindness: Specific students are recognized (by staff or other students) for their random acts of kindness.
- Kudos: Compliments are given by anyone to another person or group within our school community.

Fostering Leadership

We often talk about wanting our students to take on leadership roles in the school. We meet with parents during conferences and mention how their children have leadership potential. Well, that's great, but do we offer students the opportunity to truly lead? Sure, there are the roles of class president, treasurer, secretary, and so on. But how often do these positions lead to meaningful change in the school culture? The kind of change that the student body feels and recognizes? We can formally organize and implement school leadership programs that utilize the voice of students, parents, and teachers to make critical decisions about the way our schools function.

School advisory councils (SAC) give students, parents, and teachers authentic roles in making decisions that can impact the day-to-day operation of the school. Our middle school SAC is made up of ten elected student representatives, two teachers, two parents, and our building principal (a nonvoting member). SAC meets monthly at the high school level and biweekly at the middle school level.

Each clump (our school's name for homeroom or advisory) elects one student who will represent the group at SAC meetings. Additionally, there are two at-large student representatives. Once the SAC is established, the body elects a president, vice president, secretary, and treasurer. All students, teachers, and parents are invited to attend meetings and participate in discussions, but only those on SAC may vote.

INSTEAD, WE SHOULD BE SOLVING PROBLEMS ALONGSIDE OUR STUDENTS, INVOLVING THEM IN THE EVERYDAY COMPLEXITIES OF WHAT IT MEANS TO BE A TRUE COMMUNITY MEMBER.

One thing you'll notice is that the students hold the majority of the voting power. *What? How can you realistically hand over power to middle schoolers to make decisions about the school?* I had the same thought before joining the staff. But in reality, when students are sitting around a table with parents, teachers, and peers, they listen. They hear all of the perspectives, and though they may not always like what they hear, they consider it. Always. As a longtime teacher, I often come to the table feeling fairly certain about how I will vote on a given item on the agenda. But my mind has been changed. It happens. And it happens with parents and students as well. Some of the best, most thoughtful, respectful, intelligent, and surprising thinking has happened during SAC. I am consistently wowed by the way our students handle real decision-making with maturity, kindness, and grace. We do a disservice to our students when we try to keep things simple, make decisions for them, and clean up their mess. Instead, we should be solving problems alongside our students, involving them in the everyday complexities of what it means to be a true community member.

Implementing and maintaining a SAC requires vulnerability on the part of the school leader and the teachers. We are sharing the power, eliminating hierarchies, and leading together. We are opening ourselves up to the possibility of a change in school procedure that might make us uncomfortable. But in reality, I've found that students trust the teachers and leaders who trust them. When they are given shared responsibility—when they are seated at the table with us—they value our wisdom, and most of the time, we come to a mutual agreement that everyone can accept.

Invitation and Action Steps: *Establish a School Advisory Council*

Talk with your administrator about the possibility of establishing a school advisory council. This may look different at each grade level and school—depending on size and flexibility. Explain that the purpose of advisory council is to discuss and implement new school policies and share (and attempt to resolve) student and teacher concerns. Some steps to get started:

- Advisory council meets monthly.
- Advisory council makes decisions by reaching consensus among voting members.
- Meetings are open to the public; many students attend even if they are not voting members.
- Advisory council makes recommendations regarding scheduling, budget use, field trips, and school environment.
- Students traditionally hold four main leadership positions on advisory council: chairperson, cochairperson, treasurer, and secretary.

Sharing Our Talents and Passions

Not many teenagers enjoy talking about themselves in front of others. Far more prefer demonstrating a talent or interest. Whether it's singing, dancing, yo-yoing, delivering a comedy routine, or reciting a poem, witnessing one another's performances in school brings joy.

About four times each year, we gather for a school showcase. A committee (typically ten students and one teacher) meet throughout the month to prepare for each event. Some deliver solo performances, while others present in groups. When this initiative first began, we had the same four or five students volunteer for each showcase, but soon the number of participants grew. Those with powerful singing voices dominated the stage, until a brave young seventh grader signed up to show off his yo-yoing skills. Not only did this quiet, reserved young man receive wild applause, he also set in motion a steady stream of nontraditional performances.

We witnessed a recorder performance played through the nose, a dance routine by someone in a full-body Elmo costume, and a lightsaber battle between a teacher and student. Students played the piano, violin, and saxophone. Others performed scenes from their favorite musicals. The performances varied widely, but everyone received the same wild applause and appreciation from the staff and student body. Occasionally, someone would make it onstage only to whisper, "I can't do this." When this happened, students would shout, "You got this!" Whether the performer went through with the act or not, they received support and comfort from their peers. And yes, there were those moments when someone was awkwardly singing or dancing, and a couple of students inappropriately giggled behind shielded faces. Often, these students were called out by their peers, who reminded them to be kind.

The showcases did not miraculously make everyone friends. But the act of getting up in front of everyone required courage, and we eventually got to the point where many community members felt safe taking risks. They had witnessed far more support and kindness than ridicule. The showcases allowed our school to reveal itself as an authentic, quirky, talented group of people with widely varying interests. If nothing else, it showed everyone in attendance that hey, you can take it or leave it, but this is who we are.

Invitation and Action Steps: *Schedule a School Showcase*

Again, if you teach in a huge school, consider starting small. Organize a classroom showcase or grade-level showcase. Bring the group together and explain the purpose of the opportunity. This is a time to celebrate your talents and passions. Some things to consider as you plan for the experience:

- Involving teachers, students, and parents in the organizational and implementation process will create a greater sense of ownership.
- Decide how much time you'll allow for each performance and how much time you can dedicate to the entire showcase. Our school does these about four times per school year, and each event runs about thirty minutes.
- Two weeks prior to the event, do a run-through. It's important to preview the performances to make sure they are appropriate. It's also a time to offer suggestions and encouragement to the performers.
- To demonstrate that these need not all be performances by star singers and dancers, have a teacher volunteer to demonstrate something they enjoy—but aren't necessarily doing at a high level. For example, I like to juggle, but can only do three objects at a time.

Inviting Everyone In

Paul McCormick is a social studies teacher who lives with cystic fibrosis. One year, our community-building committee decided that, on occasion, we would offer identity presentations. During this time, students or staff could talk about their interests, what they do outside of school, and any challenges they face. Basically, it would be another opportunity to show the school community who you are.

Paul was one of the first people to give an identity presentation at our school. He started off by sharing a bit about his history of hiking, kayaking, and biking. But then he asked the students, "How many of you have heard me clear my throat during class?" All hands went up. "Well," he said, "I do that because I have a condition called cystic fibrosis." Paul went on to explain how his lungs operate differently from most people's, and he even modeled the vibrating jacket he wore each morning before coming to school. This was in no way a doom and gloom presentation; Paul interjected plenty of humor, shoveling in spoonfuls of ice cream while explaining how his condition requires him to eat massive amounts of calories each day. When he finished the presentation, students had plenty of questions, and Paul answered them honestly. This presentation led to others in the school community volunteering to share stories about their lives.

Some of the student presentations were about hobbies, sports, and activities. One student talked about becoming a competitive swimmer and the discipline it took for her to get up hours before school to train. Another student talked about her martial arts experience and then did a demonstration for the school. And on occasion, the presentations have touched on more personal topics including talks about a seizure disorder, living with cerebral palsy, and identifying as gender fluid. What struck me during each of these presentations was the reaction of the student body. What I thought might lead to problematic giggling and finger-pointing actually led to comments like, "Thank you for sharing this. I feel like I know you better now" and "I have trouble giving presentations in class about school stuff . . . it takes a lot of courage to share about yourself in front of everyone."

The reasons for giving identity talks varied. Some simply wanted others to know that they were baseball players or violinists. Sharing these passions felt good—their middle school identities were so tightly tied to these activities, they felt compelled to share. But others were tired of addressing the same intrusive questions again and again: Why are you in a wheelchair? Why do you have to ask the teacher to repeat the directions so often? Are you a boy or a girl?

Hayden suffers from epilepsy. As a sixth grader, most of her seizures were momentary and to others it appeared that she was staring off into space. These seizures happened many times throughout the day. She wanted to address the school, so her peers would stop asking her why she spaced out or seemed to ignore them so often. Hayden's mom attended the presentation to help answer questions. Now an eleventh grader, Hayden reflected on her experience:

> I would walk into school each time, and it was really hard. My eyes would flutter and kids would say, "Why are you ignoring me? Why are you looking over there? Why are you closing your eyes? Why do you look like that?" Questions like that that I didn't know how to answer at the time and made me feel

> really insecure. It was really hard to keep explaining it daily.
> When I gave that presentation, I was terrified. My hands were shaking, my palms were sweaty. There was a clock in the back that I stared at. I could not look at the crowd for the life of me. I also felt relief. There was a feeling of relief going into it. I could finally explain without feeling guilt every day going into class, feeling like I'm ignoring people.

After the presentation:

> I felt on top of the moon. Like I could do anything. People were so kind. I was met with so much love. It is one of the best feelings to know that that many people can care for you. I opened myself up and shared one of the hardest things that I've ever gone through. And with doing that, I gave so many people the opportunity to tear me down [Hayden had to pause here as she was getting emotional]. But the whole school decided that they would just build me up. And they kept saying how proud they were of me.

Hayden beautifully describes how taking an emotional risk can lead to an outpouring of love and support. Her reasons for sharing the condition benefited everyone in the school. It educated the student body and relieved Hayden of having to explain herself again and again. Still, there were some postpresentation frustrations.

"I was definitely treated with more caution—from everyone. I even saw that in teachers. I could feel it, like another eye on me." Hayden emphasized that this was a downside of giving the presentation. She didn't want to be treated with caution; she didn't want to be singled out. But when asked if she was glad she gave the presentation, there were no regrets:

> I really am. It's a big part of my story. It made me strong. It made me blossom into the person I am. And it made me be able to help others want to go up on that stage. After that, other people went up, and that felt really cool.

Samuel has cerebral palsy and spends most of his time in a wheelchair. He is one of the brightest, most outgoing, inquisitive, and talkative middle schoolers I've ever taught. When he was in fourth grade, some of his classmates were pressing buttons on his wheelchair and taking control of it from behind. To establish boundaries, Samuel decided to address the class. Later, the presentations evolved into teaching others about his condition. He's continued to do this throughout his middle and high school years. Samuel is now in eleventh grade, and I recently visited with him to learn how giving identity presentations impacted his time in school:

> There is something joyful about it. Oh! This person is going to learn about different kinds of people and their experiences. And then because of that, hopefully, their empathy and understanding of the world around them will grow.

I assumed that because Samuel performed in theatre and had given these talks so many times, the presentations were easy for him. I was wrong.

> Despite the fact that I'm very comfortable with large groups of people and talking to people, it's not always easy. I always joke that I'm a performer with performance anxiety. But, I was excited.

Samuel went on to explain more about why he feels strongly about sharing his story with groups of students and teachers at school:

> When I started giving these talks, I realized that I was part of a group. A minority group, a more isolated community. A community that has gone through some stuff. And has some history, and not always a comfortable one. We are not always included in equity conversations. So, this is an important part of my identity and I like getting to share it with people. I like seeing people's understanding increase. It's that sense of wonder that keeps me coming back and doing it again. [Some] people are frustrated by

> having to explain things, but I'm on the other end of the spectrum. When I finish the presentations it's a pretty big high most of the time. After the presentation, it makes people feel comfortable talking to you. I wanted people to know that it's [the disability] part of the identity but it's not all of the identity.

What started out as a presentation to establish boundaries and respectful behaviors among his peers has morphed into identity presentations that cultivate empathy, compassion, and connection.

Nikola entered middle school as someone who identified as gender fluid. They were frequently asked, "Are you a boy or a girl?" Wanting to be clear about their identity, Nikola, along with their mother, gave an identity presentation in front of the school. Now an eighth grader, Nikola recalls the experience:

> At my old school, I was giving small bursts to individual people of who I am, what my identity is, and why it's ok. When I came to my new school, I decided to do this one presentation to get all those individual events out of the way. Of course, I still had to tell some people individually or remind them, but that presentation really made my year a lot easier because I didn't have to give those constant reminders to people.
>
> It was definitely taxing, and I probably was not paying full attention for the rest of the day, but I was definitely really excited because I thought that it went over so well and so many people congratulated me afterwards.
>
> I know some people really respected me for being able to do that presentation, and some people were, I don't know, a little skeptical in general because of my age and my confidence in my identity. I was able to validate myself a little more because of how well and how openly everyone received that presentation and my identity. It's not like I was going to hide my identity or anything, and I think that was the best way to get it out there.

For Nikola, giving this presentation was a relief. They didn't mind individually explaining their identity to people when asked, but it was tiresome to do it over and over again. Boldly stating who they were took tremendous courage, but it reduced the overall time and energy they spent teaching others on a daily basis.

Identity talks helped the students know one another. After each session, there is often an easier feeling in the school, a greater comfort in being around one another. When the walls we put up by trying to appear the same as everyone else come down, we find a rhythm of acceptance, a feeling of compassion that pervades the community.

Invitation and Action Steps:
Offer Identity Presentations

Find a teacher who's willing to give an identity presentation to the whole school, grade level, or class. Next, invite students to do the same; emphasize that this is not required. Have interested students meet with you to discuss what they'd like to cover. If necessary, consult the student's guardian; several of our students had a parent copresent alongside them. Some things to consider when preparing for an identity presentation:

- Why do I want to share this information with the group?
- What do I want everyone to know about me?
- What questions might those in the audience have about my topic?
- Who or what do I need with me while I present?
- Will a slideshow help or hinder my presentation?
- If I have questions or concerns about how it went, who can I talk to after the presentation?

Invitation and Action Steps:
Invite Parents to Share Their Stories

We can also invite adult family members into school throughout the year to tell their own stories. Everyone benefits from hearing what it was like for parents in school, how their experience shaped who they've become, and how these memories continue to impact them throughout their lives. Not only does this bring new and unique perspectives into the classroom, it also demonstrates a willingness for parents to be vulnerable. And in turn this is guaranteed to broaden our network and strengthen the school-to-home connection.

Set up a time for parents to talk about their journeys in front of a class or school. Your invitations might outline what you are looking for; it's important to note that this would not simply be a "I worked hard to get where I am today" lecture. Rather, the presentation should focus on obstacles, struggles, failures, and successes. Some bulleted points for them to cover:

- What fears held you back from taking risks in school and work?
- Who motivated and supported you and your journey, and what did that support look like?
- What's something you've done that took courage?
- What's a fear you've overcome or are still working to overcome?
- How do you find the courage to face tough challenges? What specific tools do you use to face your fears?

Other Considerations

Establishing Boundaries: *When, What, Why, and How Much Should I Share?*

VULNERABILITY WITHOUT BOUNDARIES LEADS TO DISCONNECTION, DISTRUST, AND DISENGAGEMENT.

—BRENÉ BROWN, *DARING GREATLY*

We shouldn't be diving into vulnerability on the first day of school. Relationships need to be established before we can share deeply with one another. In her book *Daring Greatly*, Brown states,

> We don't lead with, "Hi, my name is Brené, and here's my darkest struggle." That's not vulnerability. That may be desperation or woundedness or even attention-seeking, but it's not

> vulnerability. Why? Because sharing appropriately, with boundaries, means sharing with people with whom we've developed relationships that can bear the weight of our story. The result of this mutually respectful vulnerability is increased connection, trust, and engagement. (2012, 46)

This points to the necessity of flexibility and an understanding that each of our classrooms will look different. Your community might be ready for a level of vulnerability by October, whereas mine may not be ready until December. And this will vary from year to year, from period to period, as each group of students is unique.

It may be tempting to speed things up by trying to get real, quickly. But students will know if we are forcing things, and it will be counterproductive to the work of establishing an authentic learning environment. As Brown explains, this can actually do more harm than good:

> Vulnerability is based on mutuality and requires boundaries and trust. It's not oversharing, it's not purging, it's not indiscriminate disclosure, and it's not celebrity-style social media information dumps. Vulnerability is about sharing our feelings and our experiences with people who have earned the right to hear them. Being vulnerable and open is mutual and an integral part of the trust-building process. (2012, 45)

In her book *Rising Strong*, Brown (2015) further discusses the importance of boundaries: "Setting boundaries means getting clear on what behaviors are okay and what's not okay" (123). Brown furthers her explanation here: "What boundaries do I need to put in place so I can work from a place of integrity and extend the most generous interpretations of the intentions, words, and actions of others?" (123). I like this framework, because it allows for individual comfort levels. The reality is that every classroom will look slightly different, as it should. No two teachers will carry themselves in the same manner.

During my prep periods, I used to hang out with colleagues in the hall. I didn't get much work done. Now, when a colleague knocks at my door during a prep period, I'm better at staying in my room and saying, "This isn't a good time. Can we touch base later?" I've established boundaries, so I am able to make better use of my time, and when I do chat with colleagues, I can give them my full attention.

I've established boundaries with my students as well. I love to laugh and joke with kids, and because we are so comfortable with one another, they sometimes—without an ounce of malice—will say something inappropriate or hurtful. On occasion, someone would say something about my bald head, such as "Your head is really shiny." OK, I am bald, and I have been guilty of making self-deprecating jokes regarding my dome. But that was a mistake. It encouraged kids to talk and joke about appearances. Now, I make a clear boundary. It's not OK to talk or write about one another's personal appearances. No jokes about hair, clothing, piercings, and so on. Knowing this makes the classroom a safer place. They are clear about one of my boundaries and will respect it. This builds trust and provides clarity.

In the vulnerable classroom, we are bound to face hazy lines, moments when we wonder whether we are going too far. When students choose their writing topics, what do we encourage, allow, guard against? I know that I used to be far more protective, preferring safety over risk. If I felt a student was writing about something personal, I encouraged them to choose a different topic. But to be honest, they rarely chose anything personal. Now I understand that this was due to the fact that I never modeled vulnerable writing. As soon as I began doing so, students knew it was accepted, and at times, necessary for writers to be vulnerable. For far too long, my fear over too much authenticity prevented me from cultivating the kind of writers who write with purpose. I'm sure this stemmed from my own experience as a student when there was a clear separation between school tasks and personal business—and the two rarely intersected. That way of being was further cemented by my teacher certification program, where the message was clear: Don't share your own stories, keep personal business out of the classroom, focus on the curriculum. But we need not stifle their emotions and ignore their experiences for the sake of maintaining a sterile learning environment.

WE SHOULDN'T BE DIVING INTO VULNERABILITY ON THE FIRST DAY OF SCHOOL. RELATIONSHIPS NEED TO BE ESTABLISHED BEFORE WE CAN SHARE DEEPLY WITH ONE ANOTHER.

Students need to know what they can write about and share during discussions. I don't think teachers need to provide a list of topics that are off limits in school; rather, they need to create a learning environment where students feel comfortable asking during a conferring session, "Here's what I'm thinking about taking on for this project. Do you think this will work?" Then, we can have an authentic conversation about why the student is choosing the topic and whether or not it's suitable. If necessary, guardians can be included in the decision-making process as well. We can set boundaries with our students while still allowing them to be authentic, vulnerable human beings in school.

Conferring about book selection and writing topics offers natural opportunities to build trust. Through these conversations, students realize that we are here to work alongside them as we make tough decisions. As our relationships develop and strengthen, we can begin to share our personal stories, offer heartfelt apologies when needed, and engage in conversations that require courage. Building trust is a process, and we always need to be vigilant about our reasons for sharing openly. We must ask ourselves *why* we might share a particular story with our students. If we are struggling to find an answer, we should probably hold off.

Establishing boundaries allows us to be clear about our reasons for sharing—or not. It demonstrates that we value our relationships enough to be patient, to be self-reflective, and to consider all the variables around a given topic.

Connecting at Home: *Teacher Vulnerability from a Parent Perspective*

I've shared quite a bit about how students, teachers, and school leaders can benefit from vulnerability in school, but how do guardians feel about this practice? Do they notice a change in the way their children talk about school? Do students bring home stories about vulnerable class discussions? Is there a greater sense of community and belonging in school? More risk-taking? Or is there a discomfort with all of this vulnerability stuff? Is there confusion about why this is necessary, why their children are being asked to lean into discomfort? I think it's important to inform parents of our reasons for modeling vulnerability in school.

A back-to-school letter home should include a message about vulnerability (see Appendix for a sample letter to families). Being upfront about our commitment to authenticity and risk-taking will let families know that we plan to create a safe space where students can be themselves. It's also important to emphasize that students will not be asked to share anything that makes them uncomfortable.

Vulnerability should never be forced, and though we, as teachers, may model personal vulnerability, students will move at their own pace.

After a year of modeling vulnerability in the classroom, I asked adult family members to reflect on how this school year (or past school years where vulnerability was present) impacted their child in school and at home. What follows is a sampling of their responses.

> I did get the feeling that vulnerability was the norm in Maya's English. In the past, Maya was very reluctant to share anything about her OCD or anxiety with friends, let alone acquaintances in a class setting. We, as her parents, have let her take the lead on how much she feels comfortable sharing in situations. As she gets older she has realized that there is a stigma against mental health problems as not being real, or being actual medical issues. She of course wants to help break down these barriers and help normalize discussions and considerations involving mental health problems. Only through her classes at Delta discussing difficult topics, and with other students being also brave enough to discuss vulnerable subjects, has she been able to write and convey things to teachers and classmates about her OCD. A few examples are an essay she wrote about how people shouldn't use the phrase "being OCD" about things involving neatness or in a cavalier manner in any way. Also, an essay she wrote about why she likes to read and how it is often an escape for her.

Maya was never asked to write about her anxiety, nor was she told to write about anything personal. She chose to take on this topic because she felt comfortable doing so and because she felt passionate about helping to remove the stigma from mental health issues.

> Another way that a vulnerable classroom has helped Maya, is settling her emotions. She is an emotional sponge and is so empathetic that she can feel others' emotions deeply. Sometimes she will ask me what is wrong because my face looks sad, and I'm only wishing that the weather was better or something

> so slightly negative that I can't believe she can perceive this.
> If a teacher was upset about something in the classroom, but
> didn't let the kids know about it, Maya would feel very anxious.
> Knowing what's going on is a relief to her.

The preceding paragraph speaks volumes about the hidden world of student perception. When we, as teachers, rub our face in frustration, when we raise our voice, when we dismiss a comment, students notice. They are concerned about why we are reacting this way. How often do we let them know why? How helpful would it be if we stopped and said, "Look, everyone. I'm having a rough day. If I seem impatient, it's not your fault"? This is counter to everything I learned in teacher school. There I was told, "No matter how rough your night was, you need to come to school and put on an act for your students. Fake that smile, and you can break down when the students leave." How inauthentic. This doesn't mean we should overshare or unload our problems on the students—we should never do that. But a brief and sincere statement of how we are feeling will go a long way.

> In the long run, I fully believe that responsible, thoughtful,
> self-reflective adults only get that way because they watch
> their role models and incorporate what they admire. So much
> of our cultural shortcomings stem from arrogance, unwilling-
> ness to examine ourselves, and a focus on acquiring status.
> Vulnerable teachers earn their student's respect and teach the
> power of humility.

This comment hits me in the gut. I have been guilty of playing the know-it-all teacher in the classroom. My arrogance was always a mask used to cover up my insecurities. Now I'm much more comfortable examining myself and admitting fault. I wish I was taught from early on that making mistakes in front of students was OK, that modeling the messiness of learning should be a natural part of the teaching process.

> There are still teachers who are not confident enough to practice
> vulnerability. They may do some of the dialogic work but then
> when really challenged they retreat. Those who do walk down
> the harder road are beloved and supported and because there

> is a critical mass of those teachers, the students come away strong and flexible. I do think that isolated individuals have a hard time being innovative when they do not have support from administration and other teachers.

The preceding comment emphasizes the importance of strong school leadership. When our school leaders embrace and encourage authenticity, teachers will be emboldened to lean into discomfort.

> We know many of her teachers on a more human/personal level than we did her teachers in elementary school. She [our daughter] knows more about their interests, families, and special circumstances. It seems that she has found it easier to bring the occasional concern to teachers—asking for help when there has been interpersonal conflict.

When teachers are approachable, students feel safe. When the inevitable school drama arises, students will have someone to consult. The previous comment demonstrates the importance of student–teacher connections when dealing with student-to-student conflicts.

Some guardians didn't respond to my questions, and I'll never know how they really feel about the idea of teacher vulnerability in school. But I was encouraged by the responses I did receive. They were overwhelmingly positive, and it was clear that the risks are worth it. We can never meet everyone's expectations of what a teacher should be—that is an impossible task. Some may believe we are only here to serve students a scripted curriculum and nothing more. But we know that relationships matter. When I think back to my own experiences in school, I remember the teachers, their energy, their words, their ways of being in my presence. Whether or not I learned how to become a better writer in their class was largely due to how much I trusted them to guide me. I needed to know a bit about who they were, how they felt about the books we read, the topics we discussed. They needed to be humanized. This parent says it best:

> Kids watch us like hawks and if we insist on our superiority, our perfection, our non-existent flawlessness, they know better. Vulnerable teachers by contrast, admit of their humanness, take

responsibility for the limits of their knowledge, and instill in students the urgency to make the world meaningful for their own sakes.

Humanizing Our Classrooms and Schools

I'll never forget the time a sixth-grade student walked in from recess and said, "I love sixth grade." (This happened about halfway through the school year.) I asked her why, and she said, "I don't know, I just feel like I can breathe." I needed to know more about what this meant, so I asked her to go on. "In the past, I have felt like a rubber band in school. As the year goes on, I keep getting stretched and stretched to the point where I feel like I'm going to snap. And then summer comes, and I relax. But the next year, the stretching starts all over again. This year is different. I don't feel the tension building. This year, I'm still in my summer rubber band mode." Still not satisfied, I smiled and asked her if she could explain why she was able to stay in "summer rubber band mode."

She took a deep breath and looked at the ceiling. "Even though there are still kids who might laugh at me sometimes, most students and teachers support my weirdness. I can say what I really think, write what I really feel, and everything will be OK. In fact, most of the time, people are super nice about it. I just like coming to school."

Oh, the power and joy in knowing that students look forward to coming to school. Our school and classroom culture can absolutely make or break a student's entire school year. Establishing a strong classroom and school community takes time, patience, and courage. It requires clear communication and a willingness to set boundaries. Above all else, it needs to be authentic.

LOOKING BACK   LOOKING AHEAD

Consider answering these questions in a personal journal and then discussing with a colleague:

- In what ways have you invited the voices of students when making decisions in your school and classroom?

- How can you begin to create more opportunities for students to be part of decision-making processes in your school and classroom?

- When have you given students the opportunity to take on leadership roles?

- How might you create spaces where students can lead outside of the classroom?

- In your school, are there opportunities for students to share their talents and passions?

- How can you offer opportunities for students to showcase their strengths?

- Consider a time when a student or colleague crossed a boundary. How did this impact the classroom or school community?

- How can you be clearer about your boundaries in the classroom?

- What are some brave actions you can take to invite a greater sense of authenticity?

CLOSING THOUGHTS

BE BRAVE AND BE REAL

I'll never forget my first day as a classroom teacher. After a solid student teaching experience, I came in feeling confident. But, on that first day, a student walked in and handed me a note: "Mr. Rockower," it read. "Please be sure to allow Sarah a seat near the front of the room. She has an auditory processing condition and needs to be seated near the teacher." Another note read: "Please keep your eye on Kyle. He is new to the school and doesn't know anyone." Other notes were turned in, each asking me to understand specific accommodations for their child. It hit me hard. Student teaching . . . well, that was practice. I'd had a big safety net. But now I was on my own with twenty-six humans who needed me to *know* them. To understand their conditions, their strengths, their level of ability to function independently in school. And I was only receiving notes about a few of them. Every one of them was unique, whether they walked in with a note or not. Whether there was an Individualized Education Plan attached to them or not. They were complex, changing, guarded, nervous, bold, and inquisitive. I had spent so much time preparing lessons, thinking about homework, and structuring classroom expectations, I hadn't thought enough about the slow reveal that would need to happen with me and every student in the room. That work should have been my primary focus.

My own experiences in school should have taught me how fundamental the teacher–student relationship really is. But, like so many things, we forget. We move into adulthood and forget to feel what it's like to be twelve years old, walking into school, knowing we will be at the mercy of strangers who may make or break us. We somehow think that because we endured school, today's students must do the same. As if our school trauma was a rite of passage, and was a necessary part of the process. No. Our students need not suffer similar pain to become strong, capable citizens. No matter their path, they will struggle, confront challenges, and deal with hardships. That will be part of everyone's journey. It's our job to build them up, to see everything that is good, and to continually remind them how harnessing their strengths can help them navigate these inevitable hardships. Whether it's getting through a tough writing assignment, taking deep breaths as they tackle a math problem, finding it in their heart to apologize for a wrongdoing, or sharing a perspective that differs from the majority of the class, we are supporting them with warm eyes and a compassionate heart. That, they will always remember.

Being vulnerable is contagious. Authenticity is contagious. When we demonstrate what it looks like to share our own art, model the reaction we have to powerful writing, and respectfully invite difficult conversations into the classroom, students will follow. They may not jump in with two feet, though some likely will. In time, many will join us in taking small risks. The few who don't and aren't ready will benefit from a year of witnessing others lean into vulnerability.

We always have a choice between operating from a place of fear or a place of courage. Often, I know what I *should* do, but sometimes I allow fear to get in the way. Making decisions based on avoiding fear will leave us in a sterile, unchanging world of education. We owe more to ourselves and to our students. So, consider your boundaries, make them clear, and then be real. Do the identity work, lean into hard conversations, share your art with students, and say you're sorry when you mess up. We learn from people we care about, and we can only care about them if we *know* them. Show them who you really are, tell stories, laugh, cry, and allow them to do the same.

APPENDIX

EXAMPLES OF VULNERABILITY IN STUDENT WRITING

When we as teachers model risk-taking in our own writing, it's clear that students are more willing to be vulnerable themselves. But what does this look like in practice? What types of writing do students produce when they feel empowered to take risks? For some, it may be sharing about a personal struggle or a loss, but for many students, it's not about revealing deeply personal topics. Rather, it's often about including small moments in the midst of an essay about a sporting event or a touching sentence in a vignette about a new pet. Following are excerpts from student writing that reveal both big and small risks.

Foster Care

Sarah, grade 8

> When I was 10 years old my family started foster care. At first, it was fun for me. I just had a new little kid to play with every once and a while. Just a really long sleepover. I never really realized the significance of it. Now I'm getting older. After our last placement, I found myself thinking, *How am I going to love this child knowing I have to let them go?* That's such a difficult thought to fathom at such a young age. When you're young you may lose a toy or a shirt but you never think about losing a child.
>
> It all started last summer. We had a placement with a 3-year-old girl. It was pure bliss for me. Exactly what I had always pictured. I got to be a big sister and always had a cute little kid around. Until I realized that that was the honeymoon

period. What I didn't realize was that it was never going to be perfect and that sometimes "okay" has to be enough. My family's stress level went through the roof, and we all decided she was not a good match—which turned out to be one of the worst decisions we've ever made. If we would've given it more time, it would've been okay. Yet, we thought we weren't strong enough to take it. Once we discovered that, it hurt. We felt like another burden on her journey. One more home, one more time she would feel useless. I will always remember the last time I saw her. She was wearing a little yellow romper and pig tails. I hugged her for the last time and realized I had to let go.

After that experience, we had to make changes. Changes about how everything was handled. We all just needed to adjust and communicate. It's scary to try again. We felt like failures, and we didn't want to fail another child. But we decided to give it another try, and we got our names back on the list.

Recently we've been placed with a new child. It's going well, but I can't help but think about losing her. Since I am a person who always needs a plan, I struggle with this part of foster care. I do not have the comfort of time. This is one thing you truly cannot plan. I'm scared of the uncertainty. Of what will happen next. As time goes on I start to pull away. Because the tighter I hold on the harder it will be to let go. I understand the end goal of foster care, you want the kids to go home safely. The hard part is, even though they're where they need to be, you're not. You're just left with the pain of the goodbye. You need to learn how to let go and that is why loving a foster child is so hard.

Why Do I Read?

Maya, grade 8

I read because I can.

I read to learn of the privilege that I have, and to learn how to use it to the benefit of those who need it.

I read simply because the world is full of things to feel, of things to learn, of new perspectives to understand, and I can do those things by opening the pages of a book.

I read to explore new possibilities for myself, to learn of all I could become. I read to feel the pages, to feel the wonder of what an author can do.

I read to learn about how to solve my own problems, and how to deal with myself. If protagonists, antagonists, and all in between can do it, then surely if I try hard enough, then so can I.

I read to feel things that I would not normally feel, and to expand my horizons.

I read to love myself, and to love those around me.

I read to do all of these things, and more. When I read, I become a part of the books, and the books become part of who I am.

I read to be me.

Super Bowl Victory

Nathan, grade 7

I couldn't believe this was actually happening. My dad always told me about times the Eagles made it to the super bowl but lost. In 2005, I was one year old. My dad told me that that year the Eagles played the Patriots in the super bowl, but lost 24–21. Another time they lost in the super bowl was in 1980, when my dad was just eight years old. They lost to the Oakland Raiders 27–10. So it was about the right time for an Eagles super bowl win. I was the most nervous I'd been in my life for a sport on TV. The game started off well for the Eagles. We drove down the field and kicked a field goal, putting us ahead 3–0. The patriots answered, and it was 3–3. The game went back and forth most of the half. A big turning point was when it was fourth and goal, and the Eagles called the Philly special. It was a direct snap to Corey Clement, who flipped it to Trey Burton. Burton then threw it to Foles in the end zone for a touchdown. This made it 22–12 Eagles, at halftime. Towards the end of the third it was 29–26 Eagles. I knew it wasn't even close to over because the Patriots always found a way to come back from any deficit. With about eight minutes left, I was biting my nails as we trailed 33–32. We had one last drive. Foles found Zach Ertz over the middle, and he dove across the goal line for the touchdown. We held them out, and were super bowl champions for the first time ever. We had beaten the Patriots 41–33. I was jumping and screaming with my dad, and the rest of the family. It was a day I will never forget.

I Have a Peanut Allergy

Sydney, grade 6

Everywhere I go

5 words follow me

They poke at me

Like a bug that never goes away

Everywhere I go

I have a peanut allergy

I say it to everyone I meet

Do you want to go get donuts?

Sorry, I have a peanut allergy

Do you want a bite?

Sorry, I have a peanut allergy

What do you want to eat?

I don't know, I have a peanut allergy

What would you like to order?

I'll have the spaghetti and meatballs please,

Oh,

And I have a peanut allergy

I'll tell the kitchen

Hungry

Sydney, grade 6

We are in Boston

About to go to the football game

We are with my parents' old friends

I'm having a great time

Except I didn't want to go to this restaurant

I didn't recognize the name

What if they use peanuts?

I wouldn't know

But I'm hungry

I order my burger with fries

We have to ask about the bun

To see if it's peanut safe

It is

I'm so hungry

And I'm feeling a bit better

My food comes out

We ask if the fries are fried in peanut oil

The waiter goes back in the kitchen

He comes out momentarily and says

No

I pick up a fry

Just about to put it into my mouth

Then our waiter says

But the fries do have *chunks* of peanut

My heart drops

And so does the french fry from my hand

My mind starts racing

I was about to put it in my mouth

I could have had a reaction

I'm hungry

But I do not eat for the rest of lunch

The Day I Got My Parakeet

Trent, grade 8

One day in July, my Mom, out of the blue asked if we wanted to go to Altoona to get a parakeet. Well, not completely out of the blue. We'd been discussing this for a little while, maybe a month, but it seemed like just a pipe dream. So, my little brother James, my mom, and I all got in the car to drive the hour long drive to Altoona. Nat and I were so wound up from sitting still for that long (keep in mind we were 5 and 7 at the time) that when we burst into the shop, I'm pretty sure we scared every single parakeet in there. After that commotion, my mom found an employee to help us. We found a quiet, green & yellow one with blue spots on its cheeks that we decided we loved. We also got a nice, big, cage. The employee took the parakeet and put her in a tiny, cardboard box for the journey home. Then, the naming began. Mom was all for Kiwi, but my brother and I were dead-set on Tie-Dye. We outvoted mom 2-1, and our new budgie was finally named. As we held the cardboard box that enclosed our small keet, I was touched by the life we quite literally held in our hands, as touched as I could be when one is 7.

Where I'm From

Manny, grade 6

I am from doing as many Brazilian Jiu-Jitsu tournaments as I can

from breaking my left arm when I was 8

I am from loving to learn about World War II

from enjoying the 4th of July with my family

from loving to dye my hair blue

from a family that loves to watch sports together

I am from loving to snowboard

And loving all kinds of music

I am from always trying my hardest

from a world with a few close friends

I am from Washington DC even though I didn't live there long

and from having big emotions, sometimes I am all the emotions

I am from knowing where I am from

My Grandmother

Miranda, grade 10

I was terrified of my grandmother growing up. I believed her to be a cruel and unforgiving woman—always angry without reason. She had a toxic relationship with my mother throughout her childhood, and the trauma my grandmother caused became a running joke in our family. I was constantly reminded of how lucky I was to have a "mother who loved me."

Selma was intelligent and determined; that was something I never doubted. Her knowledge of the world was extensive and her experiences extraordinary. But her behavior was almost child-like and petulant at times. She had experienced such severe trauma in her lifetime, yet she was easily agitated by such minuscule things. I had a difficult time making sense of the two women I knew. I knew the grandmother my mom cautioned others to avoid, who screamed at me in hotel lobbies, and who made me feel intellectually inadequate. But I also knew the grandma who cooked incredible Ashkenazi dinners, knit itchy (but beautifully intricate) sweaters, and helped pay for my elementary school education when we couldn't afford it.

The complexities of my grandmother's personality could have been easily justified to me, though they never were. My mother doesn't miss her mother. She was frightened of her, and they fought constantly. But something almost miraculous has happened in the last year. Nearly every day I will say or do something, and my mother will exclaim, "Oh, I wish your grandmother were here to see this. She would be so proud of you."

Gratitude Letter

Dear Mom,

Thank you for taking care of the heaps of laundry on Sunday afternoons, and having to run downstairs every time the washing machine beeps. Thank you for gourmet dinners on Saturday nights. Thank you for the hours of chopping and sizzling in the kitchen. Thank you for feeding Fozzie every morning, and letting him chase the squirrels in the yard. Thank you for playing with Pebbles when he was trapped inside his cage. Thank you for the calendars you write in, and the organization it holds, it guides me through the weeks. Without you I wouldn't remember my basketball forms or my money for Sheetz when I have away games. Thank you for letting me Maddie-fy your kitchen when I wanted to play "Chopped."

Thank you for asking if I'm warm enough in the car. Thank you for still smiling when you're having a rough day. Thank you for packing my lunches, and giving me frog and ladybug ice packs, it always puts a smile on my face. Thank you for reading me Junie B Jones in the bathtub when I was little. Thank you for helping me with my math homework. Thank you for being my second math teacher, and putting up with every tantrum I throw per math sheet. It's not your fault I don't understand. I don't know why I take it out on you. Thank you for making me laugh and having crazy days with me, sometimes I don't think we know what we're laughing about anymore. Thank you for picking me up and dropping me off at basketball practice throughout the week. Thank you for letting me talk to you about all my dumb drama.

Most of all, I want to thank you for being you. Thank you for being the mom no one else could ever be for me. Thank you for everything you do, I don't know how you do it all. I can barely do my own homework. Thank you for being my actual superhero. I'm so lucky to have you. You're like my planner. Except you don't just come with dates and notes. You come with kindness, life, love, beauty, a caring heart, and positivity. I don't think perfect should be a word. Everyone says nobody is perfect, and I mostly agree but you're pretty perfect. Without you my life would spill like the water glasses I knock over at dinner. I just wanted to thank you for everything you do. You are so special, I hope I can tell you that enough.

Love,
Maddie (grade 8)

Letter to Class

Dear Class,

On the first day of school, I mentioned some of the things that are most important to me as a teacher. At the top of the list was "building a strong community." I always want this classroom to feel like a home away from home. Many friendships have been built, and we've had some amazing conversations as a group. Just the other day, some of you suggested that I come up with an adjective to describe each of you. It was fun (and easy) thinking of positive things to say about you. When I read the adjectives aloud, you all smiled and nodded, not just about your own, but about your classmates'. This shows me that you know each other, and that even though you may not all be close friends, you recognize the positive qualities in one another.

Over the last few weeks, I've noticed an increase in cliques forming. As most of you know, cliques are groups that exclude other people. They are always together and will sometimes act superior to others. This could mean that they are huddled together all the time, at lockers, desks, etc. Or, it could go beyond that, and lead to eye rolling or making frustrated faces when they are asked to work with different people. This may seem like no big deal, but people can be (and are being) hurt by this behavior. Mean stares and gossip can cause deep wounds and make people feel badly about themselves.

Unfortunately, this is happening in our classroom and in our hallways. I cannot force you to be friends with someone, and I don't want to make you feel as though I'm doing that. Sometimes we want to be a part of a group so badly, we start acting like someone else. We lose ourselves and end up making decisions that go against our own beliefs. This is uncomfortable. It happened to me when I was in seventh grade, and I lost some really good friends, just because I wanted to be part of a more popular group. Fortunately, when I was in high school, I stopped trying to be like others and went back to being myself. I was lucky enough to regain the trust of my true friends.

I think this class can work together to repair our community that is struggling a bit right now. I'd like to invite you to write back to me. Please share some of your observations. Here are some things I'd like you to write about. Feel free to add other thoughts, if you come up with anything.

- Have you witnessed cliques that exclude?

- Have you ever felt excluded this year? If so, when?

- Have you excluded others this year? If so, why?

Everyone, please answer this question:

- What is one thing you could do that would make our classroom a stronger community?

No one will be asked to share their letters with anyone other than me. Their purpose is to help improve our classroom community. Later, we may have a discussion about your observations, but you won't need to share anything unless you'd like to.

Sincerely,
Mr. Rockower

Letter to Families

Dear Families,

Welcome to our school community! I like to think of our classroom as a home away from home. One of my goals is to make it a space where students feel free to be their authentic selves, express their opinions, and take risks in their learning. To make this happen, I need to model authenticity and vulnerability. By sharing my own writing and stories with students, apologizing when I make mistakes, and inviting crucial conversations into the classroom, I hope to foster a community of critical thinkers who take pride in their work.

While inviting real-world topics is certain to energize classroom conversations, it may also create some discomfort. This is to be expected, and leaning into that discomfort can help stretch our thinking and understanding of varying perspectives. Sometimes, this means listening to classmates share their opinions, and other times it means speaking our own truths. Please know that students will never be forced to share anything that makes them uncomfortable. As a teacher, I am here to facilitate conversations and help guide students to be better listeners, thinkers, readers, and writers. The more authentic our reading material, dialogue, and projects are, the more likely we are to cultivate student engagement—which we know leads to personal and academic growth.

If, at any time during the school year, you'd like to meet to discuss our learning, please contact me.

Best,
Mr. Rockower

REFERENCES

Ahmed, Sara K. 2018. *Being the Change: Lessons and Strategies to Teach Social Comprehension*. Portsmouth, NH: Heinemann.

Atwell, Nancie. 2017. *Lessons That Change Writers*. Portsmouth, NH: Heinemann.

BARWE. 2021. "About Us." Accessed January 14, 2021. https://www .barwe215.org/about-us.html.

Beghetto, Ronald A. 2018. "Taking Beautiful Risks in Education." *Educational Leadership* 76 (4): 18–24. http://www.ascd.org/publications/educational -leadership/dec18/vol76/num04/Taking-Beautiful-Risks-in-Education.aspx.

Bomer, Katherine. 2010. *Hidden Gems: Naming and Teaching from the Brilliance in Every Student's Writing*. Portsmouth, NH: Heinemann.

Brown, Brené. 2010. "The Power of Vulnerability." Filmed June 2010 in Houston, TX. TED video, 20:03. https://www.ted.com/talks/brene_brown _on_vulnerability?quote=870.

———. 2012. *Daring Greatly: How the Courage to Be Vulnerable Transforms the Way We Live, Love, Parent and Lead*. New York: Penguin.

———. 2015. *Rising Strong: How the Ability to Reset Transforms the Way We Live, Love, Parent, and Lead*. New York: Spiegel & Grau.

———. 2021. "Boundaries with Brené Brown." YouTube video, 5:55. Accessed January 18, 2021. https://www.youtube.com/watch?v=5U3VcgUzqiI.

Ehrenworth, Mary, Pablo Wolfe, and Marc Todd. 2021. *The Civically Engaged Classroom: Reading, Writing, and Speaking for Change*. Portsmouth, NH: Heinemann.

Frost, Robert. 1972. "The Figure a Poem Makes." In *The Robert Frost Reader: Poetry and Prose*, edited by Edward Connery Lathem and Lawrance Thompson, 439–442. New York: Henry Holt.

Hass, Chris. 2020. *Social Justice Talk: Strategies for Teaching Critical Awareness*. Portsmouth, NH: Heinemann.

Hinton, S. E. 2016. *The Outsiders*. New York: Penguin Putnam.

Kay, Matthew R. 2018. *Not Light, but Fire: How to Lead Meaningful Race Conversations in the Classroom*. Portsmouth, NH: Stenhouse.

Learning for Justice. 2019. *Let's Talk: A Guide to Facilitating Critical Conversations with Students*. Montgomery, AL: The Southern Poverty Law Center.

———. 2021. "Diversity, Equity, and Justice." https://www.learningforjustice.org/.

Lerner, Harriet. 2017. *Why Won't You Apologize? Healing Big Betrayals and Everyday Hurts*. New York: Gallery Books.

Lyon, George Ella. n.d. "Where I'm From." Accessed July 3, 2018. www.georgeellalyon.com/where.html.

Minor, Cornelius. 2019. *We Got This. Equity, Access, and the Quest to Be Who Our Students Need Us to Be*. Portsmouth, NH: Heinemann.

Ray, Katie Wood. 2006. *Study Driven: A Framework for Planning Units of Study in the Writing Workshop*. Portsmouth, NH: Heinemann.

Rief, Linda. 2018. *The Quickwrite Handbook: 100 Mentor Texts to Jumpstart Your Students' Thinking and Writing*. Portsmouth, NH: Heinemann.

Safe Space Radio. 2018. "Interview Transcript. Harriet Lerner. March 1, 2018." https://safespaceradio.com/wp-content/uploads/SSR-Extended-Harriet-Lerner-Transcript.pdf.

Thomas, Angie. 2017. *The Hate U Give*. New York: Balzer and Bray.

Williams, Alicia D. 2019. *Genesis Begins Again*. New York: Atheneum/Caitlyn Dlouhy.

Woodson, Jacqueline. 2003. *Locomotion*. New York: Puffin Books.